Celebration Press Reading

Good Habits
Great Readers™

Assessment Handbook

CELEBRATION PRESS
Pearson Learning Group

Contents

Assessment in *Celebration Press Reading* 3

Formative Assessment **6**
    Focus for Instruction 8
    Grouping Students 11
    Setting Benchmark Expectations 16

Ongoing Assessment **18**
    Opportunities in *Celebration Press Reading* 20
    Summarizing 28
    Running Record 35
    Independent Reading Behaviors Checklist 42
    Guided Reading Discussion Checklist 44
    Reading Log 46
    Checklist of Good Habits 48
    Portfolios 56

Reporting Progress **60**

Meeting Individual Needs **62**

Home-School Connection **63**

Appendix: Questions for Reading Conferences **66**

Appendix: Guided Reading Skills Checklist **74**

Bibliography/Recommended Reading **75**

The following people have contributed to the development of this program:
Art and Design: Stephen Barth, David Mager, Judy Mahoney, Elbaliz Mendez
Editorial: Adam Berkin, Jennie Rakos, Tracey Randinelli, Jennifer Van Der Heide
Inventory: Yvette Higgins
Marketing: Gina Konopinski-Jacobia
Production/Manufacturing: Karen Edmonds, Ruth Leine, Karyn Mueller, Sonia Pap

ISBN 1-4284-0395-7

Printed in the United States of America

4 5 6 7 8 9 10   10 09 08

Celebration
Press
Pearson Learning Group

1-800-321-3106
www.pearsonlearning.com
www.goodhabitsgreatreaders.com

What's the approach to assessment in *Celebration Press Reading: Good Habits, Great Readers?*

Assessment is at the very heart of *Celebration Press Reading: Good Habits, Great Readers*. It is what guides you in determining a student's reading level and identifying the skills and strategies that the student needs to master in order to advance as a reader. Once you have gauged a student's needs through assessment, the teaching material in *Celebration Press Reading: Good Habits, Great Readers* helps you match his or her needs to text and lessons.

Assessment drives instruction

In *Celebration Press Reading: Good Habits, Great Readers*, the following types of assessment assist you in matching your instruction to the specific needs of students:

- *Celebration Press Reading: Good Habits, Great Readers* assumes that early in the year teachers use a formative assessment, such as *DRA2*, to determine a student's reading level, strengths and weaknesses, reading attitudes, and interests. The richer the information the assessment provides, the tighter the link you'll be able to make between assessment and instruction. Once you have determined a student's reading level and identified needed skills and strategies, the teaching material in *Celebration Press Reading: Good Habits, Great Readers* will help you match each student's needs to texts and lessons.

- Throughout the year, ongoing, informal assessment opportunities provide you with quick snapshots of your students' progress. Our Shared Reading and Guided Reading lesson plans include many prompts and questions you can use for monitoring student progress and for informal assessment. In addition, this handbook contains background information on assessment, as well as observation forms, logs, reporting forms, and checklists you can use for monitoring student progress and for informal assessment.

- Administering a formative assessment towards the end of the year allows you to appraise the growth your students have made in their development as readers.

Small-group instruction leads to success in independent reading

- Students move through stages of reading development. To address these stages, *Celebration Press Reading: Good Habits, Great Readers* includes a range of reading material at multiple levels of instruction. The teacher's role is to identify where individual students are in their development of skills and strategies, and to provide targeted small-group instruction and multiple opportunities to read on-level text.

- The ultimate goal of *Celebration Press Reading: Good Habits, Great Readers* is to create avid, independent readers who can access and competently comprehend information from text.

What assessment support will you find in *Celebration Press Reading: Good Habits, Great Readers?*

Guided Reading Lesson Plans

Focus for Instruction An overview of the major skills and activities covered in each lesson helps you target students' needs.

During Reading Prompts provide an opportunity to assess students' reading behaviors in a supportive manner.

Assessment Checkpoint Questions help you note specific behaviors that indicate whether the student is reading competently or having difficulty with the text.

Shared Reading Lesson Plans

Focus for Instruction Descriptions of how the *DRA2* Focus for Instruction is incorporated into each day's Focus Lesson help you target your instruction.

Informal Assessment Behaviors to Notice and Check for Understanding provide opportunities for informal assessment of students' reading behaviors and their understanding of the lesson's content.

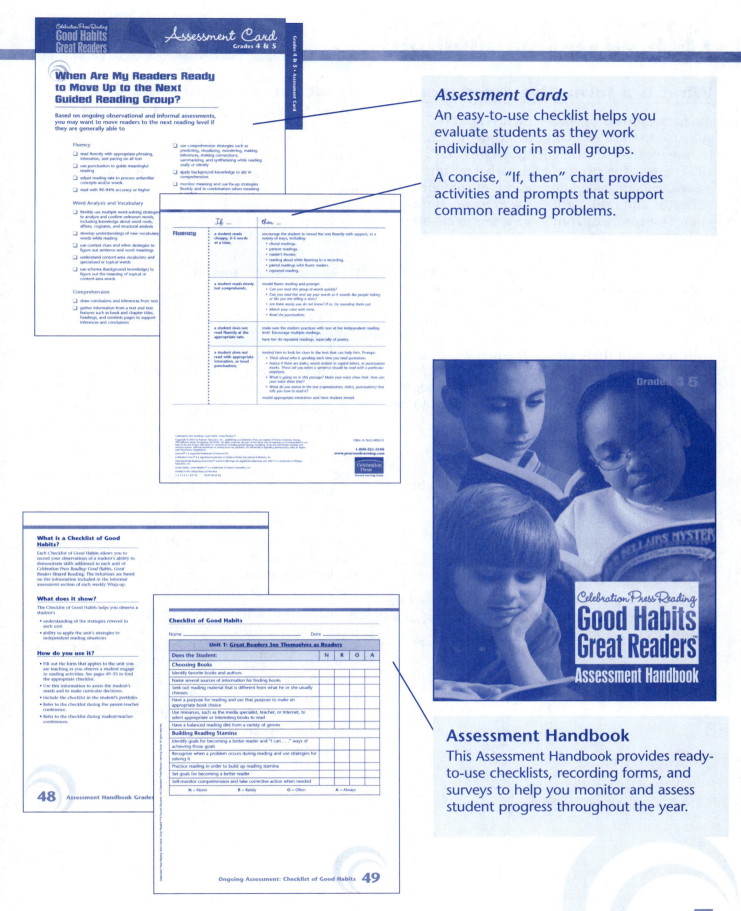

Assessment Cards

An easy-to-use checklist helps you evaluate students as they work individually or in small groups.

A concise, "If, then" chart provides activities and prompts that support common reading problems.

Assessment Handbook

This Assessment Handbook provides ready-to-use checklists, recording forms, and surveys to help you monitor and assess student progress throughout the year.

Formative Assessment

What is a formative assessment?

At the beginning of each school year, it is valuable to use a formative assessment to gather information about students' strengths and weaknesses. The strongest formative reading assessments provide information on students' strengths and needs, and serve as instructional guides for teachers. Formative assessments often yield scores in such areas as fluency rate, accuracy, vocabulary, comprehension, and word analysis, which are all important steps in reading. Diagnostic assessments, a common type of standardized formative assessments, show students' knowledge of foundation skills, such as grammar, sentence structure, and inferring, within each of these areas. Of equal value, all formative assessments provide a snapshot of a student's reading behaviors, skills, and strategies at a single point in time, enabling progress to be easily measured.

You can use the data from a formative assessment to

- make instructional decisions such as reading group formations
- determine which students may require intervention or enrichment
- identify which students share specific instructional needs
- select instructional materials that will meet the needs of each student, group of students, or an entire class

What information should a formative assessment provide?

Reading is more than a score or a level. It is a complex process that involves the integration of many sophisticated skills. The assessment that is used should, at minimum, provide information on the following:

- oral reading accuracy
- fluency, including phrasing, expression, and words read per minute
- comprehension strategies
- engagement, or insight into the student's reading experiences and interests
- metacognition, or the student's ability to reflect on his or her strengths and needs as a reader
- reflection, or the student's ability to make personal connections to text and relate new learning to known information

The most important aspect of reading assessment is listening to the student read and then discussing the text with the student. A teacher can make observations about the decoding skills a student has and has not mastered. The teacher can determine the depth of understanding a student has about a text based on a discussion with the student about it.

As teachers develop more expertise in having conversations with students, observations about a student's ability to reflect, infer, and interpret text will become clearer. The overall purpose of reading is to make meaning of the text. As students progress through the grades, the focus on reading success should shift from attention on oral reading skills to the more complex skills of comprehension.

To support instructional planning, and thereby inform instruction, a formative assessment must measure abilities on a wide range of reading skills and behaviors. The following is a general list of observable behaviors that are measured by many formative assessments. Note that not all of these areas are measured by every assessment or at every level.

Reading Engagement
- book selection
- goal setting

Oral Reading Fluency
- phrasing
- monitoring/self-corrections
- problem-solving unknown words
- accuracy
- expression
- rate (words per minute)

Comprehension:
- predicting
- summarizing: sequence of events
- summarizing: characters and details
- summarizing: vocabulary
- reflection: literal comprehension
- reflection: important idea/information

What are some examples of proven formative assessment?

One example of a formative reading assessment is the *Developmental Reading Assessment*® (DRA2), which is also a performance-based assessment that includes an opportunity for students to read aloud. *DRA2* is an individually administered reading assessment that provides insightful information about a student's strengths, needs, and overall familiarity with the reading process. The *Dominie Reading and Writing Assessment Portfolio* is another formative assessment that provides meaningful assessment information. No matter what formative assessment you choose, it is important to base the decision on the type of information you need in order to provide students with quality reading instruction.

How often should a formative assessment be administered?

Depending on the information yielded by other assessments, a formative assessment can be administered at the beginning and end of the school year in order to gain the necessary information for planning instruction and later for evaluating outcomes.

A formative assessment may also be administered several times a year to address the following:

- students who were below benchmark expectation at the beginning of the year (See the chart on pages 16–17 to help determine benchmark expectations for grades 4 and 5.)
- students who have demonstrated limited progress in reading and for whom additional information is necessary to inform instruction
- progress monitoring in schools that are required to administer an assessment three times a year
- to assess growth and re-evaluate instructional strategies for the remainder of the school year

What is the Focus for Instruction?

The Focus for Instruction is part of each *DRA2* assessment, but it can prove to be a helpful tool when connecting any formative assessment to instruction. The *DRA2* Focus for Instruction includes lists of strategies and instructional suggestions that are grouped in categories such as Reading Engagement, Oral Reading Fluency, and Comprehension. These lists of strategies and suggestions vary based on their appropriateness to the developmental stage of *DRA2*. *Celebration Press Reading: Good Habits, Great Readers* Shared Reading and Guided Reading lesson plans have been carefully aligned to specific *DRA2* Focus for Instruction items, allowing you to directly link your instruction to the results of *DRA2* or another formative assessment.

How will the Focus for Instruction help you with instructional planning?

After you administer a formative assessment, such as *DRA2*, select two to three Focus for Instruction items. Selecting too many skills usually results in a *lack* of focus, with instruction becoming diluted and, at times, ineffective. Limiting the number of items allows you to provide specific targeted instruction in the areas of greatest need. Once there is evidence that the student has made progress in these areas, other areas of instructional need can be targeted. You should also consider state and district standards, along with grade-level performance requirements, to prioritize which items to target for instruction.

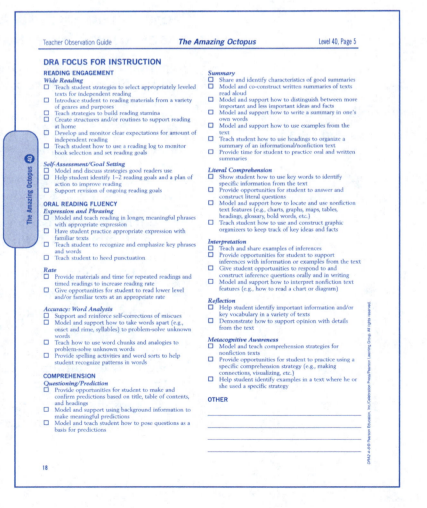

When do you observe when a student has mastered the selected item on the Focus for Instruction?

Students should begin to demonstrate increasing control over a skill or strategy after instruction and through practice. During guided reading groups, flexible reading groups, and individual reading conferences, you should monitor student progress on the targeted areas of focus for each student, always looking for evidence of improvement. Use the checklist on the front of your *Celebration Press Reading: Good Habits, Great Readers* Assessment Card to help you focus on specific reading behaviors. The checklists in this handbook will also help you keep track of student progress.

As students demonstrate more proficiency in reading and develop a deeper understanding of the reading process, there should be evidence of these strengthened skills across genres and topics. For example, students may first demonstrate competency of a skill—such as predicting—on narrative text and then transfer their ability to apply the skill to nonfiction text.

With practice, your instructional decision-making will improve, and it will become easier to

- identify the most important and appropriate Focus for Instruction items
- monitor the progress of the developing skills and strategies by identifying evidence of growth
- select texts that are the most supportive for teaching the needed skills and strategies

When is it appropriate to select new items from the Focus for Instruction, and how do you make that selection?

Becoming adept at determining student progress comes with experience, coupled with professional development. Often grade-level teams meet to create rubrics and benchmarks for student success. Gathering input from colleagues about assessment data is a powerful part of professional development. With experience and guidance, it becomes easier to see the relationship between student-learning needs and instructional strategies that will scaffold a student until he or she reaches the next level of proficiency.

Once a student is able to demonstrate understanding of the previously targeted skills from the Focus for Instruction across genres and across settings (for example, moving from a guided reading setting to confidence in independent reading), it is time to select other strategies for your instructional focus.

The easiest way to select two to three new areas for instructional focus is to refer back to the results of the most recently administered *DRA2* or other formative assessment. Again, always look for the areas on which the student received the lowest scores. More challenged readers are likely to have several low-scoring areas. Stronger readers may have few (or no) scores below the independent or proficient level. This does not mean that there is nothing on which to focus instruction. You should then focus instruction on moving the student from the proficient or independent level to the advanced level. Once the student is scoring mostly in the advanced levels, you can also work with the student on more challenging texts.

How do lesson plans in *Celebration Press Reading: Good Habits, Great Readers* link to the Focus for Instruction?

Shared Reading Lessons

In the Shared Reading lessons, a pacing guide shows how each week's Focus Lessons correlate to *DRA2* Focus for Instruction skills. *DRA2* skills addressed in each lesson are indicated in an easy-to-access chart format. (See page 4 for more information.)

Guided Reading Lessons

In the Guided Reading lessons, information on the front page of the lesson clearly describes the link between the lesson and specific *DRA2* Focus for Instruction skills. (See page 4 for more information.)

What are *DRA2* levels?

When *DRA2* levels are referenced in *Celebration Press Reading: Good Habits, Great Readers*, the designation refers to the levels of the Benchmark Assessment Books used in the *DRA2*. In the case of *DRA2*, a student's level refers to the text level at which that student is capable of reading independently. Once you have determined each student's independent reading level, you can help guide their independent reading selections. In addition to Shared Reading and Guided Reading instruction provided in *Celebration Press Reading: Good Habits, Great Readers*, your students should be reading a total of 30 to 40 minutes a day from books at their independent reading level. Reading at their independent level builds students' fluency, comprehension, stamina, and most importantly, their confidence.

There are other leveling systems, such as that developed by Fountas and Pinnell (1999). Leveling systems typically use several factors when assigning different levels to texts. Some of the text characteristics that are considered include:

- format of the book
- vocabulary
- text structure
- length
- complexity
- concept load

While there are always some skills in which a student is weaker than others, benchmark levels provide you with a common comparison of student skills based on a variety of texts with characteristics that become more complex as the levels increase. *DRA2* and other leveling systems assist you in choosing appropriate texts that match the instructional needs of each reader.

How should you group your students for reading instruction?

Upper-grade classes often have a wide range of reading abilities. All students will benefit from small-group reading instruction systematically delivered through guided reading. On-grade level students still need focused skills work. Small-group work provides differentiation of the reading curriculum and is very beneficial in the upper grades.

Opportunities for partner and group work abound in *Celebration Press Reading: Good Habits, Great Readers* lessons. Of course, Guided Reading lessons are rooted in small-group instruction; however, even the program's Shared Reading lessons promote group work through best practice routines, Talk Together (see Guided Reading Discussion Checklist, p. 45), and Apply the Strategy. Determining how to best group students for instructional purposes can be done in a variety of ways.

Use assessment to determine grouping

What students know compared to what they need to know are the fundamental bases for grouping students for skills instruction. Ideally, you want students to read with 90–94 percent accuracy (at their instructional level) while practicing a new reading skill or strategy.

The best way to assess what students know is through observation and performance-based assessing. Have them read silently and then recount either verbally or in written form important information, ideas, or thoughts. Use folders or binders and note cards or sticky notes to develop an ongoing record for each student.

The following suggestions will provide focus for your observations:

- Make notes regarding the student's attitude toward and interest in reading. (See *DRA2*.)
- Make notes regarding the student's interaction with the text, including the illustrations, diagrams, and photographs.
- Evaluate and note how well the student summarizes the text. (See Summary Rubric, p. 31.)
- Record how well the student can discuss the text.
- Keep track of what the student chooses to read. (See Reading Log, p. 47.)
- Note how the student behaves when he or she meets an unfamiliar word or concept.
- Periodically document how well the student reads by observing and recording oral reading behaviors. (See Running Record, p. 39.)
- Conduct reading surveys and interest inventories to gain further insight into students' feelings about reading and the types of stories or articles that might interest them. (See *DRA2*.)

Collecting this type of evidence is invaluable to teacher-driven assessment. Teachers employ these methods to practice reflection and observation of student performance. If *DRA2* was used as the formative assessment, you have a record of each student's independent reading level. To form guided reading groups, move students to the next level after the independent level. In addition, pay special attention to the specific areas of need on the *DRA2* Continuum and Focus for Instruction.

Assign students to flexible groups based on their needs

With 25–35 students in a classroom, each with different experiences and levels of ability, it is essential to group students for a common purpose: reading instruction. However, rather than assigning students to stagnant groups for the duration of the year, with no room for growth or movement, it is necessary to define flexible groups that change with the purpose, the task, and the reading level of the students. For instance, in addition to grouping students at specific *DRA2* levels, you may sometimes want to group students with similar interests or social needs for a particular reading activity, or for more intensive instruction on a specific strategy. When grouping students according to strategy instruction, interest, or social skills, take into account the *DRA2* levels of the students. Choosing a text that might be easy for some students ensures access to print for all the group members.

Select Texts to Match Students' Abilities and Needs

"[When matching readers with books,] always keep in mind the readers and ask yourself, 'What is this book about? What will make it easy? What will make it challenging?'" (*Guided Reading: Making It Work* by Mary Browning Schulman and Carleen daCruz Payne, 2000)

Grouping to Meet Students' Needs	
Grouping Pattern	**Instructional Purpose**
DRA2 Level (Guided Reading Groups)	To teach specific skills and strategies to students with similar achievement levels
Strategy/Skill Instruction	To work with students who need instruction on a specific reading strategy, such as making predictions or making connections
Interest	To provide an opportunity for students with a common interest to learn together
Social Skills	To give students an opportunity to build and practice skills for collaboration and cooperation

How can you use a student's instructional reading level to form guided reading groups?

An instructional level usually refers to a student's ability to read a text with 90–94 percent accuracy with some understanding of the text. It is this information that provides the most guidance for you regarding which students should be grouped together for guided reading groups. You can determine a student's instructional reading level by selecting texts that are one level higher than the student's independent reading level. When assessing with *DRA2*, instructional support should focus on any scores on the *DRA2* Continuum that fall within the instructional or independent columns. The chart on pages 16–17 shows the correlation between skills acquisition and *DRA2* levels, and should be used for reference.

The key to building an efficient guided reading group is to carefully match the student to texts that offer enough challenge to focus the student's attention without being too difficult. All students should be able to access the text so that the focus skill can be taught. For example, if students all need instruction and practice with predicting, the text used for that skill should include two key features:

- It should feature a good example of the focus skill being taught.
- It should be at the appropriate *DRA2* level so that all students can read the text.

All the *Celebration Press Reading: Good Habits, Great Readers* Guided Reading lesson plans are organized by *DRA2* level and reading skill to support your creation of targeted guided reading groups. In addition, each lesson plan identifies challenging features of the text.

Additional Considerations When Matching Students With Texts

"Considering whether a child is reading at his or her level during guided reading requires more than just looking at the text level of the child and the reading level of the text. We must consider factors within the child, such as interest and prior knowledge, as well as the type and amount of instruction and support we can provide." (*Classrooms That Work: They Can All Read and Write* by Patricia M. Cunningham and Richard L. Allington, 2003)

When might you want to form more flexible reading groups?

There may be times when you wish to form flexible reading groups that include students at different instructional levels. For instance, if you form a reading group based on similar interests, you can use the *DRA2* level to guide students' selection of texts related to that interest. Or, you can use the *DRA2* Continuum to teach a particular skill to students who need additional instruction in that area, and then have students apply the targeted skill to text at their appropriate *DRA2* level. This approach can also be used when you form reading groups for fostering social skills. (See the chart on page 12.) You will also be forming flexible groups when you group students during the Talk Together sections of the Shared Reading lessons. Literature discussion groups are another type of flexible grouping.

How do you know when to move a student up or down a level in guided reading?

In guided reading groups, teachers should track student progress in several areas. The following questions might be asked about the student's current level as the decision to move up a level is being considered:

- Is the student able to monitor his or her own understanding?
- Does the student use a variety of strategies when encountering an unknown word?
- Does the student make self-corrections quickly and easily?
- Can the student retell or summarize what he or she has read?
- Can the student apply newly learned comprehension strategies to more complex, higher-level texts?

When considering whether to move a student down a level, make the same observations as noted above, but pay attention to students who are not demonstrating success in these areas. There are students who will require more practice before they gain control of one or more of these skills. By moving down a level, students will be using text that is less complex, and that can make it easier to acquire the needed skills and strategies.

Whether moving a student up or down, it is best to provide instruction to groups of students with similar needs. Students learn from one another and instruction can be specifically targeted.

Using your *Celebration Press Reading: Good Habits, Great Readers* Assessment Card, along with careful tracking of student progress through informal assessment, anecdotal notes, and observations in guided reading groups, will support professional decision-making as you consider changing a student's text level.

How do leveled texts help you meet the instructional needs of students?

The use of leveled texts along with assessment information affords teachers the opportunity to create an instructional path that is just right for each student.

Leveled books offer many instructional benefits for improving reading instruction and enhancing reading development. Leveled texts

- offer varying levels of reading difficulty, which can be matched to a student's needs
- create opportunities to match student interests to a wide variety of topics across multiple genres
- provide opportunities to teach specific skills and strategies that build lifelong learners, such as predicting, summarizing, making inferences, drawing conclusions, and so on
- contain words that offer opportunities for word analysis skills to be used for direct instruction during guided reading or in one-on-one discussions for more challenged students
- provide text that can be read and reread to build confidence and develop fluency
- provide opportunities for teachers to model strategies for book selection that students can use when selecting books independently

All of the Guided Reading book collections in *Celebration Press Reading: Good Habits, Great Readers* consist of leveled text.

How many leveled books should a student read before moving up a level?

Once the student's independent level has been determined, the student needs a great deal of practice reading at that level. Some experts say that students should read and reread as many as 40–50 leveled texts at the independent level before moving up a level. Some of this reading will take place in guided reading groups, while other opportunities will be provided during independent reading time. At later stages, where the texts are longer, the number of texts read at a level may be fewer.

In reality, students usually have confidence and control over texts in a range of levels, based on the level of text difficulty, their personal experience, and their interests. Students may move up a level much more quickly with effective strategy instruction at their appropriate reading level. This move should be flexibly decided for each student, not for a group of students.

What are the benchmark expectations for student progress?

The chart on pages 16–17 can help you determine the skills and strategies that students should be expected to know as the school year progresses. Use the chart to assist you with end-of-quarter or marking-period assessments.

Setting Benchmark Expectations

Student Expectations by...

	GRADE 4	GRADE 5
Phonics	• Uses blends to decode unknown words. • Uses syllables to decode unknown words. • Uses base word and then suffix to decode unfamiliar multisyllabic words. • Uses word segmentation and syllabication to understand unfamiliar words.	• Uses decoding strategies appropriately and automatically when encountering unfamiliar or unknown words. • Uses knowledge of affixes and morphology to read and understand unfamiliar words.
Fluency	• Reads most ideas as meaning units. • Uses commas and quotation marks as a guide to read with expression. • Temporarily pauses to ponder the meaning of the text while decoding. • Reads silently for 20–30 minutes. • Is self-motivated to read for pleasure.	• Reads ideas as meaning units. • Uses conventions of print to guide expressive, well-paced reading. • Reads many unknown or unfamiliar words automatically. • Reads silently for 30–40 minutes. • Is totally absorbed while reading any genre.

	DRA2 Level 40	DRA2 Level 50
Vocabulary	• Recognizes that words have more than one meaning. • Begins to understand how to connect background knowledge to subject-specific vocabulary. • Identifies base words and affixes while inferring the meaning of unfamiliar words. • Uses some new words read while recounting and summarizing text. • Uses context of sentence to infer the meaning of unfamiliar words.	• Recognizes author's use of figurative language. • Connects background knowledge to subject-specific vocabulary. • Uses base words and affixes to determine the meaning of complex words. • Uses synonyms interchangeably with unfamiliar and content-specific vocabulary. • Uses context of sentence (definition, restatement, or example) and author's use of words and summarizes the passage to infer the meaning of unfamiliar words.
Comprehension	• Previews text and generates several reasonable predictions and questions related to the text of various genres. • Recounts important information from the text. • Understands the text's message and can state or write supporting details to defend his or her thinking. • Makes inferences based on explicit and implicit information from the text. • Compares text read to other texts. • Compares information while reading nonfiction text to similar information. • Uses the author's description to visualize the setting and characters. • Identifies information from graphs, charts, tables, and maps.	• Previews text, sets a purpose, and generates several thoughtful predictions and questions related to the text of various genres. • Recounts important information using the details and vocabulary from the text. • Uses purpose for reading to take notes, recording important information. • Thoroughly understands the text's message and can state or write supporting details to defend his or her thinking. • Compares and contrasts different points of view. • Chooses books effectively for a variety of purposes. • Selects, monitors, and adjusts reading strategies. • Describes the importance of setting and characters within text. • Distinguishes fact from opinion. • Makes inferences based on information from graphs, charts, tables, and maps.
Summarizing	• Writes a summary that includes most of the important information, vocabulary, characters, and some details. • Writes a summary that is loosely organized. • Writes a summary that hints at the theme of a story or the important idea(s) from nonfiction text.	• Writes a summary that includes all of the important information, vocabulary, characters, and details. • Writes a summary that is organized in a sequential order. • Writes a summary that includes the theme of a story or the important idea(s) from nonfiction text.
Rate (WPM)	Oral Reading = 105–135 WPM Silent Reading = 150–200 WPM	Oral Reading = 120–145 WPM Silent Reading = 175–225 WPM
% Accuracy	96–100%	96–100%
DRA2 Level	40	50

Ongoing Assessment

What is ongoing assessment?

Ongoing assessment is classroom-based and helps you monitor how a student is progressing toward achievement of specific skills. It occurs throughout the school year and may take the form of observations, running records, portfolios, inventories, conferences, surveys, and self-assessments.

What information does ongoing assessment provide?

Student learning improves the most when instructional strategies become more targeted and focused. Conducting informal assessments provides the data you need to continually revise and redirect your teaching to match the instructional needs of students. More importantly, ongoing assessment provides you with the valuable information you need to adjust the instructional focus of guided reading lessons.

Ongoing assessment provides the following:

- a record of changes in student reading behaviors since the last administration of the *DRA2* or other formative assessment

- more precise insight into a student's skills and strategies in reading

- specific direction for instructional planning based on observations

- interval comparisons to benchmark expectations (see pp. 16–17)

- opportunities to spend one-on-one time with a student to discuss reading

- critical information that guides daily instruction in guided reading groups

- information to guide whole-group instruction during shared reading

- insight into reading strengths and weaknesses, a student's prior knowledge about a topic, and gaps in his or her understanding

Notes you've jotted down or recorded on assessment forms during ongoing, informal assessment provide evidence of a student's progress in specified skill areas and are also a valuable resource when discussing a student's growth with parents during conferences.

Questions to Guide Observations for Intermediate Grades

- Can the student recall or summarize what is read?

- Can the student engage in a meaningful discussion with others about a given text?

- Does the student appear interested in reading?

- Does the student appear to have a good attitude about reading?

- How does the student choose books?

- Does the student read an entire book or keep changing books?

How do you conduct ongoing, informal assessment?

As opposed to formal standardized assessments, informal assessments, such as Running Records, summarizing, and conferences, need to be conducted with students in one-on-one situations. You will find some opportunities to conduct these assessments during guided reading groups when students are reading their books. The ideal time to administer these assessments, however, is during independent reading.

Much of your informal assessment data will also come from the times you are not providing direct instruction, and therefore have opportunities to record your observations of students. Good teachers are "kid-watchers" who continually observe students throughout the day. In *Celebration Press Reading: Good Habits, Great Readers*, ideal times to informally observe students reading and discussing text include the following:

- Shared Reading: During the Talk Together and Apply the Strategy sections of the Focus Lesson
- Guided Reading: In the During Reading section of the Guided Reading lesson
- Independent Reading: Ongoing

As you observe students in whole-class and small-group situations, take brief anecdotal notes and complete checklists, including the ones provided in this Assessment Handbook.

Don't try to observe every student each day. Focus on one or two students per day. Spend more time observing your struggling readers over each two-week period of time. Higher-achieving readers need ongoing assessment, but observation can be done less often.

As you observe students, take notes. Keep a different record for each student. Some teachers prefer to use sticky notes or adhesive labels to record observations. They then transfer these to a permanent record for each student. Others

choose notebooks or single sheets of paper. The goal of the recording is to answer the questions you set forth for that particular observation period. Also note observations about students that you find interesting or noteworthy. Over time, you will develop the ability to collect the most useful information pertaining to each student.

It is important to review your observation notes. Ask yourself if your notes are telling you what you want to know. Are they providing answers to the questions you are asking? The results of your observations can help you make instructional decisions. You will be able to set goals for each student. The key to successful observing is having a systematic way to observe students reading and writing each day.

Make Observation Realistic and Revealing

"When specific questions are used to guide observations, the information they reveal can be powerful; however, they can be overwhelming if you try to focus on too many at once. We suggest using one or two questions at a time to make observation both realistic and revealing." (*Reaching Readers: Flexible and Innovative Strategies for Guided Reading* by Michael F. Opitz and Michael P. Ford, 2001)

Where can you find opportunities for ongoing assessment in *Celebration Press Reading* Shared Reading Lesson Plans?

The Shared Reading lessons present significant opportunities for monitoring a student's growth in acquiring specific skills.

During the Talk Together and Apply the Strategy portions of each lesson, you can monitor a student's growth by listening in on student conversations, providing supportive prompts, and asking questions as needed. This kind of informal observation and assessment provides valuable information that can help you determine a student's ability to verbalize and apply the lesson's focus skill or strategy. Once you know whether a student understands the major points of a lesson, you can plan appropriate future instruction.

Talk Together
Working in pairs, students verbalize and apply the modeled strategy. Critical-thinking prompts and discussion questions are presented in a bulleted format. Student interaction further develops students' understanding of the lesson content. You can monitor students' thinking and reasoning by listening to them express their points of view.

Apply the Strategy
Once students have learned and practiced a day's focus strategy, they are given the opportunity to apply it, using a different piece of text. As in Talk Together, critical-thinking prompts and discussion questions help you direct and focus students' thinking and understanding.

2 · Focus Lesson
Using Text Structure to Make Predictions

Lesson Objectives
- To understand how the organization of a text can be used to make predictions
- To identify text structure and use it to predict the type of information a text contains

Materials
- Text the Teacher Needs: *In the Mountains* by Judy Bagshaw, pp. 11–15
- Text the Student Needs: Student Reader, Vol. 1, pp. 6–7, 9–11, 16–24 (*Taste of America* by Melissa Whitcraft)

Introduce the Strategy
Point out to students that texts are organized in a variety of ways. A biography might be organized by time order; a book about volcanoes might be structured around causes and effects; a book about national parks might present main ideas and details. Challenge students to think about why it is important to pay attention to text structure. Help them to realize that once readers figure out how a text is organized, they can [...] based on how that structure unfolds [...] that when the structure of a text ma[...] they can use it to make sound predi[...] them better understand the text the[...]

Model the Strategy (see [...])
Use pages 11–13 of *In [...]* model how to use text [...] predictions. Begin by r[...] scanning pages 12–13. [...] structure on those pag[...] mation to make predict[...] ter. For example, you might [...] first give a description of mountain [...] eral, followed by pages with specific [...] groups of mountain people. Record [...] concept web on the board (see con[...]

Talk Together
Have partners discuss your predictions and confirm whether or not they are correct based on the structure of the text. Begin by reading aloud pages 12–13 of *In the Mountains*. Offer prompts such as the following to help partners confirm the predictions that you made:
- *The introductory discussion on page 11 provided general information about mountain communities. What details do you learn in these next two pages that expand on the introductory discussion?*
- *What kind of a text structure do you notice being developed?*

Then read aloud pages 14–15:
- *Think about the last two pages in the chapter. How do they fit into the text structure of the entire chapter?*

Review and Reflect
Have partners share some of the ways that they con-

68   Unit 2 · Great R[...]

Professional Development
Modeling in Action
The following example can help you prepare to model today's Focus Lesson:

When I start a new chapter, I like to take a look at how it's organized so I can make some predictions about what I will read. [Read aloud page 11.] This first page seems like an introduction to the chapter—it gives general information about people in mountain communities. When I look over the next two pages [pages 12–13], I notice details about people who live in the mountains of Bhutan and Bolivia. Based on this, I think that each page following the introduction is going to give me details about a different mountain community—and there are probably even more pages about other communities to come. So this chapter is structured with general information followed by specific details. That makes sense! Recognizing how the text is structured helps me predict what will probably come next.

Note that skimming and scanning, or quickly looking over a text, is an important skill that students can use to gain insight into the way a text is organized. Remember that many books use a variety of text structures.

When using text structure to predict, it's important for students to focus on the type of information that they will encounter rather than specific content.

The structure of a text must seem logical to students if they are to make valid predictions about what will come next.

Apply the Strategy
Have students read the introduction to *Taste of America* on pages 9–11. Then ask them to look through pages 16–24 and use text structure to predict what kind of information a reader might find in this part of the book. You may wish to point out that this book is organized like *In the Mountains*, with a general introduction followed by pages of details. Have students record predictions on a concept web. Students might label the center circle *American Foods* and the outer circles *Details About Northeast Foods* and *Details About Southeast Foods*. Circulate, using prompts and questions to help students apply the strategy:
- *Think about pages 9–11. What general information did you learn about food in America?*
- *Look through pages 16–24. Will these pages give general information about American foods or details about different regions? What makes you think that?*
- *Do you think that understanding the text structure of these pages might help you to make predictions about the information in the rest of the book? Why or why not?*

Have partners compare their predictions. Encourage them to go back and read pages 16–24 to confirm the predictions they made.

My Notes

Week 1 · Making Predictions   69

The weekly Wrap-up section provides a second opportunity for informal assessment. Observable behaviors that indicate a student's use of the strategy explored during the week are listed under the heading *Behaviors to Notice*. The metacognitive questions under the heading *Check for Understanding* help you ascertain whether a student understands the importance of the strategy. Monitoring students' reading behaviors and ability to explain why a strategy is helpful provides useful input for assessing growth and designing ongoing instruction.

Informal Assessment

Behaviors to Notice

- Does the student activate prior knowledge to make predictions about a text?
- Can the student identify text structure and use it to make predictions about the kind of information contained in a text?
- Can the student identify text features that are useful in predicting and use them to make valid predictions?

Check for Understanding

- *What experiences have you had that can help you make predictions about this part of the text?*
- *How can you use text structure or text features to make a prediction about what you will learn on these pages?*
- *How can making predictions help you better understand a text?*

Related Reading

Guided Reading Lessons GR 2 Level 40

The Ancient Ones: The Anasazi of Mesa Verde, Steven Otfinoski

Hurricane, Maureen Haselhurst

Seeing Is Not Believing, Jeffery B. Fuerst

Reteaching

- In the middle of a concept web, write the name of a nonfiction text that students are about to read. Then display the cover of the text, and have students use the title, the cover image, and their own prior knowledge to make predictions about the book. Add students' predictions to the web. Next, have students copy onto sticky notes the predictions they think are most likely to fit the text. As students read, have them place the notes in the text at the point where the predictions can be confirmed. Students can revise the predictions as necessary by writing new sticky notes.

- Students may have difficulty identifying the structure of a nonfiction text. Support students by providing a list of possible text structures that may apply to the text, such as time order, description with general information and details, cause/effect, comparison/contrast, or problem/solution. Have students use the list to help determine the structure of the text and then make predictions based on that structure. Record their predictions on the board. Encourage students to check the predictions after they read.

ESL/ELL Support

- Have students work with a partner when reading a nonfiction text. Partners can look through the book for features such as photographs, diagrams, and graphs or charts. Encourage them to build a vocabulary for predicting by talking about what they see in each feature. Partners can take turns describing what they see. Encourage students to use the text features, their own prior experience and knowledge, and the vocabulary they developed during the discussion to make predictions about the text.

Week 1 • Making Predictions 73

Behaviors to Notice questions assess reading behaviors that signify mastery of the week's major strategy.

Check for Understanding questions require students to verbalize the usefulness of the strategy covered in the week's lessons or to make connections between the strategy and the text or themselves.

Together, Behaviors to Notice and Check for Understanding questions assess students' understanding of and ability to apply the focus strategy.

Where can you find opportunities for ongoing assessment in *Celebration Press Reading: Good Habits, Great Readers* Guided Reading lessons?

Ongoing assessment is a feature of the program's Guided Reading lessons. Opportunities for assessment are included in the During Reading portion of the lesson, as well as in the Discuss the Text, Assessment Checkpoint, and Writing sections of each lesson.

Discuss the Text Students' responses to questions requiring application of major reading strategies provide an opportunity for you to assess their ability to apply these skills and to determine areas in which they need additional instruction.

Guiding the Reading

Day 1 (pp. 3–17)

In This Section Curtis is unhappy about spending three weeks helping his grandparents move into a house in the Nevada desert. Then Curtis discovers a hidden letter from a great-uncle, and he and his sister, Faith, develop a whole new interest in the Nevada desert.

Before Reading

Focus Attention
- Ask students to read the book title and tell what this mystery story is about. (a hidden letter) Ask: *What clue to the possible location of a hidden treasure does the cover art give you?*
- Point out that mystery is a popular genre. Ask: *Why do you think people like mysteries so much? Do you usually figure out the mystery before the author reveals the solution?*
- Tell students that this mystery is set in Nevada. Locate Nevada on a map. Explain that many people went west in the early days of this country, hoping to find gold.
- Begin a discussion about mining. Point out that mining is the process of taking minerals, such as gold and silver, out of the earth. Ask students to share what they know about the California Gold Rush.
- Have students read the contents page and look at the illustrations in the first two chapters to preview the book. Invite them to predict what they will learn about the treasure. Have students read to find out what the mystery is and how it is solved.

Vocabulary
- Invite students to guess the meaning of *to stake a claim* (p. 15) from the following sentence: *The miner decided to stake a claim to the land by putting a sharp post into the ground.* Lead students to understand that *to stake a claim* means "to demand one's right to ownership of something." Invite pairs to write their names on a sticky note and to stake a claim on a favorite part of the classroom by putting the sticky note in that area.

Other Words to Know
- **kin** (p. 10): "family; relatives"
- **panel** (p. 9): "a section of a door that is raised or sunken"
- **pouch** (p. 9): "a sturdy bag used to carry things"
- **sagebrush** (p. 5): "a bushy plant with sweet-smelling leaves"
- **spike** (p. 9): "a large, strong nail"

Understand Plot and Mood
Remind students that when they read a story, they should follow the most important events from beginning to end. These events are part of the plot. In a mystery story, a mood of suspense builds as the plot unfolds. Use pages 3–5 to model understanding plot and mood:

Most authors of fiction begin by introducing the main characters and the setting, presenting the problem, and establishing a mood. On the first few pages, I read that Curtis and his sister, Faith, are visiting their grandparents at an isolated house in the Nevada desert. These are the main characters and the setting. When Curtis calls the area "the dullest place on Earth" (p. 5), this establishes a mood of boredom. I think the author will introduce the story problem soon.

The action will build, called rising action, as the main character tries to solve the problem. The rising action ends with the climax, which is the most exciting point in the story, and where the problem is usually solved. Then the author will wrap up the story and bring it to an end in the resolution. I'll look for all these parts of the plot as I read.

Distribute the reproducible on the back cover. Ask students to think about the characters, the mood, and the problem that is presented as they read the first two chapters of the book. Have students begin to use the reproducible.

During Reading

Prompt for understanding, as appropriate. Possible prompts include the following:
- *How does the author's choice of words help you identify Curtis's mood at the beginning of the story?*

During Reading Students' responses to prompts help you monitor their general reading ability and growth, along with their understanding of the featured skill.

- *What is the problem in the story? How does knowing the problem help you to understand why the characters act as they do?*

After Reading

Understand Plot and Mood
Discuss with students how the mood changes from boredom in Chapter 1 to excitement in Chapter 2. Then have students share their entries on the reproducible for the beginning of the story. Make sure that students identify the problem the characters face—solving clues to find the treasure.

Discuss the Text

Analyze Character Point out that readers learn about Grandma through what she says and does. Ask students to turn to page 5 and reread the last paragraph. Discuss Grandma's words and actions. Have students infer from these clues what she is like.

 Visualize Remind students that Faith called their grandparents' house "an odd old house" (p. 4). Ask students to picture the house in their mind and to write a paragraph describing things they would find there. Encourage students to draw what they visualized and to use labels in their drawing.

Assessment Checkpoint
- Can the student identify the story problem?
- Can the student describe one of the characters?

Day 2 (pp. 18–34)

In This Section When Grandma and Grandpa drive their grandchildren to the ghost town where the great-uncle had a barbershop, they find another clue to the treasure. Then they visit Grandpa's friend Sam, who takes them through a silver mine on his land. On the way home, Curtis realizes that a black car he has seen several times is following them.

Before Reading

Focus Attention
- Recall with students that the story characters have a map and clues, but they don't know what the clues mean. Invite students to use the titles of Chapters 3 and 4 to predict how the characters will try to solve the problem.
- As students read, ask them to think about the clues the characters find and how these can help them solve the problem. Have students predict what the treasure will be.

Vocabulary
- Remind students that the ghost town had been abandoned by people who moved away when the mines closed. Ask students what they think *abandoned* (p. 31) means. ("deserted, or left alone") Ask students to suggest items that might have been abandoned along with the town. (old toys, clothing, broken furniture)

Other Words to Know
- **extracted** (p. 32): "removed; taken out of"
- **sledgehammer** (p. 32): "a large, heavy hammer with a long handle"
- **timbers** (p. 31): "large pieces of wood used in building"

During Reading

Prompt for understanding, as appropriate. Here's one possible prompt:
- *Think about events that have happened so far. What do you think will happen next?*

After Reading

Understand Plot and Mood
Remind students that the rising action includes the characters' actions as they try to solve the mystery. Ask what clues the characters have found so far. Then have students fill in the middle section of the reproducible.

Assessment Checkpoint Informal assessment occurs at the end of each day. Prompts help you note specific behaviors that indicate whether the student is reading competently or having difficulty with the text.

Writing A short writing assignment requires students to apply one of the lesson skills. By evaluating students' ability to appropriately complete this task, you can monitor students' progress in understanding the targeted skill or strategy and their ability to express themselves in writing.

Discuss the Text

Understand Humor Ask a volunteer to read aloud page 32 from "After the miners drilled . . ." to ". . . and everyone laughed again." Discuss what made Curtis's remark humorous. (He used a pun or play on words.) Ask students what this scene tells them about Curtis.

 **Visualize** Have students use the illustrations and the author's description of the walk through the silver mine to write three sentences about what a silver mine would look, smell, and feel like.

Assessment Checkpoint

• Can the student describe the mood of Chapter 4?

• Can the student summarize the events that make up the rising action?

Day 3 (pp. 35–48)

In This Section Sam figures out the last clue. Then Curtis taps the wall map and opens a secret panel that leads to a silver mine under the house. The mystery of the black car is also solved: Geologists want to buy the rights to the land in order to mine its silver.

Before Reading

Focus Attention

Have students use the titles of Chapters 5 and 6 to predict how the story will end. As students read, ask them to look for answers to the questions they have about the treasure.

Vocabulary

• Ask students to tell the meaning of the word *vein* (p. 46). They may mention the vessels in the body that carry blood. Explain that *vein* has other meanings. In mining, a vein is "a crack or seam in rock that is filled with a different material." A *vein* of silver or gold may run through rock for a great distance. Ask students to locate veins in their hands or arms. Then ask:

How is a vein in your body similar to a vein of silver or gold in rock? (The vein runs through other material that surrounds it.)

Other Words to Know

• **lode** (p. 47): "an accumulation of a mineral deposit found in rock"

• **nuggets** (p. 39): "small, solid lumps"

• **stern** (p. 45): "serious"

During Reading

Prompt for understanding, as appropriate. Possible prompts include the following:

• *How does the author help you get to know Sam?*

• *What are the most important events in solving the mystery?*

After Reading

Understand Plot and Mood

Have students complete and discuss the third section of the reproducible. Ask them to point out suspenseful scenes in Chapters 5 and 6. Encourage them to identify the climax. Then invite students to discuss whether the book has a satisfying ending.

Discuss the Text

Make Judgments Remind students that Grandpa decides to sell the mining rights to his property. In order to keep the house from being destroyed, it must be moved. Ask: *Do you think Grandpa's decision was right or wrong? Why do you think so?* You may wish to make a T-chart of why the decision was right or wrong.

 **Visualize** Have students review pages 40–41 and visualize what the basement looked like. Ask them to write a short paragraph describing the basement. Invite students to draw a picture of what they visualized.

Assessment Checkpoint

• Can the student describe the climax of the story?

• Can the student track the plot from beginning to end?

How can you use the Assessment Card to monitor student progress?

The four-page Assessment Card provides a framework for ongoing observational and informal assessment. The Assessment Card addresses developmentally appropriate concerns related to fluency, word analysis and vocabulary, comprehension, and retelling ability. The checklist on the cover will help you assess a student's abilities and determine when the student is ready to move up to the next *DRA2* level. The remaining pages provide valuable suggestions for targeting instruction to specific deficiencies.

Celebration Press Reading
Good Habits Great Readers

Assessment Card
Grades 4 & 5

Grades 4 & 5 • Assessment Card

When Are My Readers Ready to Move Up to the Next Guided Reading Group?

Based on ongoing observational and informal assessments, you may want to move readers to the next reading level if they are generally able to

Fluency
- [ ] read fluently with appropriate phrasing, intonation, and pacing on all text
- [ ] use punctuation to guide meaningful reading
- [ ] adjust reading rate to process unfamiliar concepts and/or words
- [ ] read with 90–94% accuracy or higher

Word Analysis and Vocabulary
- [ ] flexibly use multiple word-solving strategies to analyze and confirm unknown words, including knowledge about word roots, affixes, cognates, and structural analysis
- [ ] develop understandings of new vocabulary words while reading
- [ ] use context clues and other strategies to figure out sentence and word meanings
- [ ] understand content-area vocabulary and specialized or topical words
- [ ] use schema (background knowledge) to figure out the meaning of topical or content-area words

Comprehension
- [ ] draw conclusions and inferences from text
- [ ] gather information from a text and text features such as book and chapter titles, headings, and contents pages to support inferences and conclusions
- [ ] use comprehension strategies such as predicting, visualizing, wondering, making inferences, making connections, summarizing, and synthesizing while reading orally or silently
- [ ] apply background knowledge to aid in comprehension
- [ ] monitor meaning and use fix-up strategies flexibly and in combination when meaning is unclear
- [ ] interpret author's message by reading beyond literal interpretations
- [ ] sustain comprehension through stretches of longer text
- [ ] answer literal and interpretative comprehension questions by connecting schema, information from the text, inferences, and synthesis

Retelling
- [ ] recall and summarize facts and details of the text and restate them orally or in writing in an organized manner
- [ ] use text vocabulary when retelling
- [ ] use details from the text and personal experience to support opinions
- [ ] use story grammar or story structure (character, setting, goals, problem, solution, and outcomes) to retell the story with appropriate inferences and judgments

Checklists provide a way to assess whether students are generally competent in a skill area and are ready to move up to the next instructional level.

Competency in major reading skill areas is assessed in order to monitor a student's growth and readiness to move to the next instructional level.

The "If...then..." format allows you to quickly locate a skill and find a suggestion to help a student who lacks competency in that skill.

What If My Readers Are Having Trouble?

	If ...	*then ...*
Word Analysis	a student cannot analyze a word,	prompt him to use multiple strategies to problem solve the word. Ask: • What is the first syllable? • What is the first chunk? • What are the first two letters (blend)? • Does this look like a word you know? • What is the beginning (middle, ending) sound? • Do you see a chunk that you know? • Did you read to the end of the sentence then go back to the word and try again? • Do you know the prefix and/or suffix? • Do you know the meaning of the word root or base word? • Do you know a word like that?
Vocabulary	a student has trouble understanding more challenging vocabulary words,	make sure that the student understands an oral definition of the word, presented in terms the student already knows. Provide students with a familiar synonym. assist the student with additional • word maps • contextual analysis lessons • structural analysis lessons, including prefix, suffix, and root/base word instruction
Comprehension	a student reads so slowly that she cannot comprehend,	assist the student with prereading activities such as • choosing books at appropriate independent and instructional reading levels. Frequently, this problem indicates the text is above the student's reading level. • building background. • activating prior knowledge. • filling in KWL charts. • completing an Anticipation Guide. • providing think-alouds. • rechecking for appropriate fluency rate. See Fluency activities, back page.

	If ...	*then ...*
Comprehension	a student reads quickly with little comprehension,	prompt the student to adjust her reading rate to help her grasp difficult or confusing parts of the story. encourage the student to use self-monitoring strategies with prompts such as • Does it make sense? • Does that fit with what you already know about that topic? • Is that what you thought would happen? • Does it look and sound right to you? • Something wasn't quite right. What was it? • Would ____ fit there? • What section was hard to understand? • Why was this part hard to understand?
	a student has difficulty applying the target strategy,	model how to use the strategy again, using a different text. encourage students to understand the purpose of the strategy using prompts such as • Why would you use this strategy? • How can this strategy help you understand?
	a student cannot retell/summarize,	make sure the student • knows how to retell and what is expected in the retelling. • understands how to identify the main idea or purpose and supporting details. • understands that he must put pieces of information together while reading to make sense of text. • is constructing meaning while reading by using imagery, predicting what might happen, and using self-monitoring strategies appropriately. • understands story grammar and structures of narrative text, including setting, characters, goals, problems, and solutions. • understands characteristics of nonfiction text.

Once you've assessed a student's abilities in various reading skill areas, the Assessment Card provides prompts and concrete teaching suggestions.

What will you find in this Assessment Handbook to help keep track of student progress?

This Assessment Handbook contains many ready-to-use assessment tools that can help you monitor student progress on an ongoing basis. These tools are specifically designed to support the instructional philosophy and approach you will find in *Celebration Press Reading: Good Habits, Great Readers* Shared and Guided Reading lessons.

Ongoing Assessment Tools			
Tool	**What It Does**	**When to Record?**	**Page Number**
Summary Rubric	Assesses student's comprehension	Repeat every 2–4 weeks for struggling readers; every 8–10 weeks for readers on or above grade level	31
Story Frame	Supports student's identification of important elements of a fiction selection	Use when introducing summary writing, and with students who need extra support	33
Text Frame	Supports student's identification of important ideas in a nonfiction selection	Use when introducing summary writing, and with students who need extra support	34
Running Record	Assesses student's comprehension, fluency, and word-solving strategies	Repeat every 2–4 weeks for struggling readers; every 8–10 weeks for readers on or above grade level	39
Independent Reading Behaviors Checklist	Assesses student's ability to select, read, and comprehend text independently	Repeat every 8–10 weeks until mastery is attained	43

Ongoing Assessment Tools continued			
Tool	**What It Does**	**When to Record?**	**Page Number**
Guided Reading Discussion Checklist	Assesses student's speaking and listening skills during Guided Reading participation	Repeat every 8–10 weeks until mastery is attained	45
Reading Log	Keeps a record of books a student has read independently	Ongoing	47
Checklist of Good Habits	Assesses student's understanding and use of the strategies taught in each Shared Reading unit	Use as each Shared Reading unit is completed	49–55
Portfolio Selection Slip	Helps student self-evaluate items placed in his or her portfolio	Ongoing	58
Portfolio Checklist	Keeps a record of items placed in a student's portfolio	Ongoing	59
Home Reading Record	Keeps a record of books a student has read at home	Ongoing	64
Guided Reading Skills Checklist	Keeps a record of skills featured in Guided Reading lesson plans	Ongoing	74

How can you use summaries to monitor ongoing student progress?

Summaries are used in *DRA2* to evaluate a reader's comprehension and understanding of a story. During the school year, summaries can continue to assess whether or not a student understands a story.

When students summarize a story, you gain insight into their understanding of story structure and their proficiency with language. Ongoing assessment can involve evaluating written summaries that students prepare after reading a text or listening to and making observations about students' oral summaries.

When you notice a breakdown in comprehension, you may have the student revisit the text, perhaps walking through the book page by page or paragraph by paragraph, recounting information in order to facilitate a greater understanding. This process should support the student's ability to summarize. If necessary, you can ask probing questions to scaffold the student.

Why should you use summaries on an ongoing basis?

Using summaries on an ongoing basis and as part of your regular instructional routine helps students by

- teaching them to pay attention to the key elements of text, such as characters, settings, supporting details, and specific vocabulary
- providing a model for talking about texts in a meaningful way
- providing practice in sequencing the events of texts or other events
- making connections between their predictions (tentative meaning) and their understanding
- providing a means for students to demonstrate their progress in understanding and restating or summarizing the key points of more complex texts

Monitoring students as they learn to summarize orally provides support for writing summaries at higher levels of the *DRA2* or in other settings. One effective strategy for supporting students who struggle with writing summaries is to ask the student to do more oral summarizing.

Post the elements of a good summary on the classroom wall, and refer to it as you or the students summarize (see chart below). As a student's skills improve, you should see more thorough and detailed summaries across curriculum areas.

Always remember to provide positive feedback after summarizing attempts, specifically labeling the element that is being complimented. For example, *I'll bet that using the name of the main character when you summarized helped you better remember the book,* or *Including the main idea and key details in this nonfiction summary was a great idea.*

You will find specific lessons on writing summaries in Unit 2 of Shared Reading and in the Guided Reading teaching plans.

A Good Summary Includes . . .

- Important information from the text

- Supporting facts and details

- Insights or inferences that may stem from connections or prior knowledge

- Important text vocabulary and proper nouns, where applicable

- Student's own language

- Events and/or important information in an orderly and logical sequence

What are the criteria for teaching guided versus independent oral and written summaries?

Before using summaries for assessment, teach and model the skill. Then allow students opportunities for practice. The following instructional routines can be followed.

Guided Summaries

- Read a short passage aloud to students.

- Use a chart or other graphic organizer to model as you summarize the passage. Model your thought process aloud, explaining why you are including or excluding particular details as well as how you are determining the structure of your summary. Emphasize the more complex plot points and character relationships.

- Then read another passage aloud to students. Ask students to answer the following prompts:

- Narrative prompts:

  Where does the story happen? How is the location or time frame important to understanding the story?

  Who is the most important character?

  What is the character's problem?

  Who are the other characters in the story? What is their relationship to the main character?

  How does the most important character solve the problem? How does he or she receive support from the other characters?

  How does the story end? Is the ending realistic?

  What did you learn from the story?

- Nonfiction prompts:

  What are the key ideas and facts?

  What are the important details?

  What key words were important?

  What did you learn? How is this related to other content or information you already know?

  What details did you leave out? Why?

This process may be repeated with small groups or individual students.

Independent Oral and Written Summaries

- Read a passage aloud to students, or ask them to read a printed version of the passage.

- Tell students to remember important information and/or events that they hear or read.

- Provide students with opportunities to practice summarizing the passage both in small groups and individually. You can prompt them with questions such as *What happens next?* or *Did you forget anything?*

How can a Summary Rubric help you assess a student's ability to summarize?

A Summary Rubric like the one on page 31 allows you to evaluate a student's summary using criteria that measure comprehension, understanding of reading strategies, interaction with the text, and language development. The rubric on page 31 is designed to be used with both fiction and nonfiction texts. Administer the Summary Rubric to students periodically to ensure that they are summarizing skillfully.

Summary Rubric

Use this rubric to help you assess a student's ability to summarize a fiction or a nonfiction text.

Name _____ Date _____

Directions: Use checkmarks to assess the student's summary.

The summary exhibits:
3 = Excellent comprehension of the text and its components
2 = Moderately good comprehension of the text and its components
1 = Minimal comprehension of the text and its components
0 = Limited or no response; significant misinterpretation of the text and its components

Summary	3	2	1	0
[1] Recounts important information from text				
[2] Includes supporting facts and details				
[3] Includes insights or inferences that may stem from connections or prior knowledge				
[4] Includes important text vocabulary and proper nouns, where applicable				
[5] Uses student's own language				
[6] Summarizes events and/or important information in an orderly and logical sequence				

How do you interpret the results?

Items 1–2 assess reading comprehension.

Item 3 assesses reading strategies and textual interaction.

Items 4–6 assess complex language development.

How can a Story Frame or Text Frame help students write summaries?

Summaries can be an integral part of a setting that fosters more complex language development through an interaction with printed words. A Story Frame like the one on page 33 can scaffold students to write summaries by helping them identify the structures and conventions of a narrative text. A Text Frame like the one on page 34 can do the same for a nonfiction text.

- Have students read a selected passage. Ask students to try to remember important information and/or events that they read.

- If students are reading a fiction passage, provide them with a copy of the Story Frame on page 33. If the passage is nonfiction, provide them with a copy of the Text Frame on page 34.

- Have students complete the appropriate frame and use it to help them write their summaries. Then use the Summary Rubric on page 31 to assess their written summaries.

Story Frame

Use this story frame to identify important elements of a fiction selection.

Name _____   Date _____

Title _____

Author _____   **Genre** _____

Setting (Time and Place)	**Main Characters**

Major Events in Order (or Major Events That Set Up the Problem, Lead to the Resolution, and End the Story) (*Use the back of this paper if you need more space.*)

_____

_____

_____

_____

_____

_____

_____

Text Frame

Use this text frame to identify important ideas in a nonfiction selection.

Name _____ Date _____

Title _____

Author _____ **Genre** _____

Chapter Title or Subhead 1:_____
Main Idea of This Section: _____
_____
_____

Chapter Title or Subhead 2:_____
Main Idea of This Section: _____
_____
_____

Chapter Title or Subhead 3:_____
Main Idea of This Section: _____
_____
_____

Chapter Title or Subhead 4:_____
Main Idea of This Section: _____
_____
_____

How can a Running Record help you monitor and assess students' progress?

A Running Record, which is called the Record of Oral Reading in *DRA2*, is an assessment tool that measures students' fluency, rate of reading, accuracy of reading, and comprehension. When done consistently over time, Running Records can be used to assess students' reading development and achievement.

While administering a Running Record, you observe a student reading and note any reading errors. You record what the student reads aloud. Miscues, or deviations from text, are not only noted, but also analyzed. Based on your analysis, you make inferences about how the student processes the text in his or her attempt to derive meaning. You can conclude whether or not the student uses meaning sources, language structure, and/or visual word patterns when encountering new or unfamiliar words.

Good readers self-monitor and self-correct as they read. On Running Records, you take note of students' self-correction strategies. Running Records can be used to help you analyze a student's reading ability and tailor curriculum to his or her needs. They also allow you to provide the student with text that is appropriate for his or her development.

How do you select text for Running Records?

Since books read by students in intermediate grades are much longer than books read by early readers, it is not necessary for students to read an entire book or chapter. However, the passage read should be at least 100 words in length. This will provide a sampling of errors and self-corrections large enough to direct further instruction.

The text should be one that students have not previously read. If a selection is too easy, you will not have enough opportunities to analyze

miscues. Similarly, if a text is too difficult for a student, he or she will likely become frustrated and not read at his or her personal best.

How do you administer a Running Record in the classroom?

After you have selected an appropriate text, you are ready to administer the Running Record. You should assess one student at a time. Make sure you will not be interrupted during the assessment. Other students should be involved in independent activities. Some teachers prefer to sit next to the student so they can closely monitor his or her behavior. Explain to the student the purpose of the Running Record. Help relieve any anxiety by telling the student you want to listen as he or she reads. Be sure to explain that you will be taking notes to help you remember how well he or she read.

As the student reads, use specific notations, or codes, to record both the words read correctly and the miscues. There are two ways to do this. Some teachers make a copy of the text being read. They mark the miscues on it as the student reads. Others use a blank Running Record form, such as the one on page 39. Using the same linear arrangement as the text, you can record the correct reading and miscues on the form.

You should also add personal notes to the Running Record. You may make notations about the reader's attitude, behavior, and understanding. It is important to time the reading in order to determine the student's reading rate. Finally, you can have the student retell the text in sequence to assess his or her comprehension.

In general, you should administer a Running Record for each student once every eight to ten weeks. Administer a Running Record more frequently to struggling readers—as often as every two to four weeks.

How do you record miscues on a Running Record?

The codes for miscues are somewhat standard, allowing for comparisons across classrooms. The chart below provides a concise reference for coding miscues.

Coding Chart			
Miscue	**What It Is**	**Coding**	**Example**
Accurate Reading	Student reads word correctly	No notation	The cat is huge.
Omission	Student skips a word	"word"	The cat is (huge).
Insertion	Student adds an extra word	^	really ^ The cat is huge.
Substitution	Student says a different word than the one in the text	hug huge	hug The cat is huge.
Self-Correction	Student makes an error and then corrects it unprompted	SC	hug/SC The cat is huge.
Repetition	Student repeats a word, phrase, or sentence	R	R The cat is huge.
Reversal	Student reads words in reverse order	cat⁄is	The cat⁄is huge.
Sounding Out	Student sounds out a word in segments	hu|ge	The cat is hu|ge.
Word Told by Teacher	Student is told what the word is by the teacher	T huge	T The cat is huge.
Long Pause	Student pauses at length between words	W The cat or The | cat	W The cat is huge. or The | cat is huge.

How do you interpret the miscues?

In addition to the miscues included on the chart on page 36, you should observe specific types of errors and self-corrections the student makes and make notations about your observation of each error and self-correction. These observations can help you understand the strategies the student uses correctly and those strategies that the student needs to acquire or improve. For each error and self-correction, record an *M* to indicate a meaning cue, an *S* to indicate a language/structure cue, or a *V* to indicate a visual cue.

Errors

- If the error (for example, a substitution) makes sense in the given context, record an *M* by the error. This is an indicator that although the student made an error, he or she is using meaning cues while reading.

- If the error sounds right in the sentence or is the same part of speech, record an *S* by the error. This is an indicator that the student is using syntax, or structural cues, as he or she reads.

- The error can show the student is using both meaning and structure. In this case, record both an *M* and an *S* by the error.

- If the error looks like the word in the text, record a *V* by the error. This indicates the student is using visual cues as he or she reads.

- Mispronunciations still get credit, but not if there is a major difference in pronunciation that renders the word unrecognizable.

Self-Corrections

When a student self-corrects, it is important to determine what made the reader recognize and correct the error.

- If a student makes a self-correction because the original meaning was incorrect, record an *M* to indicate the student is using meaning cues as he or she reads.

- If a student makes a self-correction because the word didn't sound right in the sentence, record an *S* to indicate the student is using syntax, or structural cues, as he or she reads.

- If a student makes a self-correction because the word didn't look like the actual word in the text, record a *V* to indicate the student is using visual cues as he or she reads.

How do you score a Running Record?

Self-corrections and repetitions are coded each time but never counted as errors. An error on a proper noun is coded each time, but it is only counted once as an error—the first time the error is made.

To determine a student's reading accuracy, follow these steps:

1. Count the number of words in the passage.

2. Count the number of errors.

3. Subtract the number of errors from the total number of words. This gives you the number of words read correctly.

4. Divide the number of words read correctly by the number of words in the passage. You will get a percentage. This percentage is the student's accuracy rate.

How can a Running Record help you determine a student's independent reading level?

For a student to achieve success with instructional reading of a text, the accuracy rate should be about 90–94 percent. When a student reads a Running Record text with a 90–94 percent rate of accuracy, you know that the student is reading at the appropriate instructional reading level. You can then go one level higher to provide the student with appropriate guided reading instruction.

Running Record

Use this form to note miscues and observations as you administer a Running Record.

Name _____

Date	Text Level	Title	Accuracy	WPM	Notes on Phrasing, Expression, Miscues, etc.

Reminders: Accuracy is determined by dividing the number of words read correctly by the number of words in the selection.

_____ words correct ÷ _____ words in selection = _____% accuracy

Words per minute (WPM) are figured by dividing the number of words in a selection by the number of seconds it takes the student to read, then multiplying the product by 60.

_____ words ÷ _____ total seconds = WPS × 60 = _____ WPM

What are some other examples of tools for ongoing assessment?

Reading Journal

Reading journals are places where students reflect on their reading independently, with the teacher, or with other students. Reading journals help you better understand your students' interests and abilities. Providing time for journal entries gives students a chance to respond to what they have read and learned, how it relates to them personally, how they learned it, how they used it, and what they feel they still need to learn.

Many entries of fluent readers will consist of sketches, notes, and reflection. Students' entries may include notes on reading problems, things students feel they do well as readers, questions they have about themselves as readers, when they may apply a strategy in the future, and what made them attempt a particular strategy. Journals may also include notes on story elements, such as plot, literary technique, and author's purpose, or on connections, visualizations, and inferences made.

As you and the student share and discuss journal entries, you can observe such things as comprehension strategies the student is using and the student's reading preferences and attitudes. Comparing a student's reading journal entries over time presents an opportunity for you to take note of student progress and tailor daily instruction.

In *Celebration Press Reading: Good Habits, Great Readers* Guided and Shared Reading, students use reading journals in a variety of ways. See pages 28–29 in the frontmatter of the Shared Reading Teacher's Guide for a complete description of how to use reading journals to support the program.

Reading Conference

Many teachers regularly schedule a one-on-one conference with each student. You can use this time to talk about literacy learning, gain insight into a student's attitudes, and view his or her progress and achievement. You learn about a student's instructional and motivational needs. What you learn during a conference can help you plan for future instruction.

You can also hold a conference centering on a specific text. In this instance, you introduce a text to a student. The student reads the text independently and then has a short conference with you to discuss his or her reading. The conversation can include a discussion about the text itself, whether or not the student understood what was read, and whether or not the student found the text challenging, interesting, and informative.

Regular conferences should occur with all students, but they need not be lengthy discussions. You are checking in, observing, and making notes of key points to remember about a student's reading progress. Struggling readers will need more frequent contact and observation.

You can use the Check for Understanding and Behaviors to Notice questions in the Wrap-up section of the Shared Reading lessons along with the prompts on the Assessment Card to guide your conferences and assess students. The lists of prompts in the Appendix of this handbook (pp. 66–73) correspond to the *Celebration Press Reading: Good Habits, Great Readers* Shared Reading units of study. Taking notes at each conference and referring to notes you took previously will help you compare and document the student's skill development over the course of the school year.

Self-Assessment

A self-assessment requires a student to monitor and evaluate his or her own learning. *DRA2* includes reading surveys that monitor a student's reading preferences, habits, and goals, as well as his or her awareness of strategy use.

In Shared Reading, the Check for Understanding questions in each weekly Wrap-up section informally assess a student's ability to understand, apply, and explain the reading strategies he or she is using. As students respond to these metacognitive questions, note if they begin to use the language of strategy instruction. For example, do students use terms such as *predicting, making connections*, or *making inferences*? Do they understand how using these strategies will help them as a reader? Do they share examples of how they sometimes reread to clear up confusion? Do students talk about having reading goals? Do they speak about favorite books and authors?

Portfolios are another type of self-assessment. Pages 56–59 of this Assessment Handbook provide information and forms to help you use portfolios in your classroom.

What is an Independent Reading Behaviors Checklist?

The Independent Reading Behaviors Checklist on page 43 allows you to write your observations of a student's independent reading behaviors as he or she progresses throughout the school year.

What does it show?

The Independent Reading Behaviors Checklist helps you measure the student's

- book selection strategies
- book preferences
- text engagement
- reading habits

How do you use it?

- Complete the form as you observe how a student interacts with text.
- Use this information to assess the student's needs and to make instructional decisions.
- Include the checklist in the student's portfolio.
- Refer to the checklist during the parent-teacher conference.
- Refer to the checklist when conferring with the student.
- Complete the checklist periodically to monitor progress.

Independent Reading Behaviors Checklist

Use this form to assess a student's independent reading behaviors.

Name _____ Date _____

Behavior	AN	S	M	A
Book Selection				
Selects books that are at the right level				
Knows what he or she likes to read				
Sticks with a book until it is completed				
Requests (or purchases or checks out from the media center) new books to read				
Reads a variety of authors and genres				
Other:				
Other:				
Other:				
Engagement				
Stays in one place during independent reading				
Reads a selected text during independent reading				
Discusses books with classmates or the teacher				
Chooses to read when work is completed				
Reports reading at home				
Other:				
Other:				
Other:				

AN = Almost Never   **S** = Sometimes   **M** = Most of the Time   **A** = Always

What is a Guided Reading Discussion Checklist?

The Guided Reading Discussion Checklist on page 45 allows you to write your observations of a student's speaking and listening skills as he or she participates in a guided reading session or literature discussion group. It also allows you to measure the student's progress throughout the school year.

What does it show?

A Guided Reading Discussion Checklist helps you observe the student's

- ability to contribute higher-level thinking to a discussion
- comfort and ease with speaking and listening for varying purposes
- engagement in group-learning situations

How do you use it?

- Assess only one or two students during an individual guided reading session.
- Complete the form as you observe each student participate in the guided reading discussion.
- Use the information to assess the student's needs and to make curricular decisions.
- Include the checklist in the student's portfolio.
- Refer to the checklist during the parent-teacher conference.

Guided Reading Discussion Checklist

Use this form to record observations of a student's participation in guided reading discussions.

Name _____ Date _____

During guided reading discussions, the student ...	AN	S	M	A
voluntarily contributes pertinent information				
helps move the discussion along				
encourages other students				
shows an understanding of text vocabulary before it has been formally introduced				
makes predictions using the text, text features, and background knowledge				
connects the text to things he or she has read, seen, or experienced				
can explain inferences he or she has made using information or examples from the text				
asks insightful questions to help infer, predict, and summarize				
asks questions to clarify confusions				
can easily and effectively summarize what has been read using his or her own words plus important text vocabulary				
appears to comprehend the text at a deep level as evidenced by comments				
AN = Almost Never **S** = Sometimes **M** = Most of the Time **A** = Always				

What is a Reading Log?

The Reading Log on page 47 is used to chronicle and evaluate what a student is reading. The log is completed by the students themselves; you can use each student's log to track his or her reading habits, interests, and stamina. The log shows the student's reading history.

What does it show?

A Reading Log helps you understand:

- how many pages a student reads daily
- how long it takes a student to read a book or text of a particular genre
- how well a student can evaluate his or her reading experience

How do you use it?

- Have students list the title, author's name, and genre of each book he or she reads daily during independent reading.
- Ask students to circle the number that best describes how they'd rate what they read: 1 being the lowest rating, 5 being the highest.
- Include the log in the student's portfolio.
- Refer to the log during the parent-teacher conference.
- Refer to the log during student-teacher conferences.

Reading Log

Name _____

Dates Read	Title and Author	Genre	How Would You Rate What You Read?
Date(s) _____ Pages read _____			Didn't Like It Really Liked It 1 2 3 4 5
Date(s) _____ Pages read _____			Didn't Like It Really Liked It 1 2 3 4 5
Date(s) _____ Pages read _____			Didn't Like It Really Liked It 1 2 3 4 5
Date(s) _____ Pages read _____			Didn't Like It Really Liked It 1 2 3 4 5
Date(s) _____ Pages read _____			Didn't Like It Really Liked It 1 2 3 4 5

What is a Checklist of Good Habits?

Each Checklist of Good Habits allows you to record your observations of a student's ability to demonstrate strategies addressed in each unit of *Celebration Press Reading: Good Habits, Great Readers* Shared Reading. The behaviors are based on the information included in the informal assessment section of each weekly Wrap-up.

What does it show?

The Checklist of Good Habits helps you observe a student's

- understanding of the strategies covered in each unit
- ability to apply the unit's strategies to independent reading situations

How do you use it?

- Fill out the form that applies to the unit you are teaching as you observe a student engage in reading activities. See pages 49–55 to find the appropriate checklist.
- Use this information to assess the student's needs and to make curricular decisions.
- Include the checklist in the student's portfolio.
- Refer to the checklist during the parent-teacher conference.
- Refer to the checklist during student-teacher conferences.

Checklist of Good Habits

Name _____   Date _____

Unit 1: Great Readers See Themselves as Readers				
Does the Student:	**N**	**R**	**O**	**A**
Choosing Books				
Identify favorite books and authors				
Name several sources of information for finding books				
Seek out reading material that is different from what he or she usually chooses				
Have a purpose for reading and use that purpose to make an appropriate book choice				
Use resources, such as the media specialist, teacher, or Internet, to select appropriate or interesting books to read				
Have a balanced reading diet from a variety of genres				
Building Reading Stamina				
Identify goals for becoming a better reader and "I can . . ." ways of achieving those goals				
Recognize when a problem occurs during reading and use strategies for solving it				
Practice reading in order to build up reading stamina				
Set goals for becoming a better reader				
Self-monitor comprehension and take corrective action when needed				

N = Never   R = Rarely   O = Often   A = Always

Checklist of Good Habits

Name _____ Date _____

Unit 2: Great Readers Make Sense of Text				
Does the Student:	**N**	**R**	**O**	**A**
Making Predictions				
Use prior knowledge to make predictions about a text				
Identify text structure and use it to make predictions about the kind of information contained in a text				
Identify text features that are useful in predicting and use them to make valid predictions				
Asking Questions				
Formulate text-explicit questions and locate the answers within a text				
Formulate text-implicit questions and use text clues and prior knowledge and experience to answer those questions				
Formulate questions that help him or her wonder about and anticipate information or events				
Ask questions to clear up confusion				
Identify the author's purpose based on questions he or she would like to ask the author				
Respond to questions he or she has asked as answers emerge in the text				
Make predictions based on questions that anticipate information or events				
Clarifying				
Resolve confusions by discussing them with a reading partner				
Reread and/or read ahead to clarify understanding of the text				
Consult an appropriate reference source, when needed, for clarification				
Draw from prior knowledge to clarify concepts				
Summarizing and Synthesizing				
Pause throughout a text to paraphrase				
Turn a heading into a question and identify which ideas answer it				
Identify how a group of ideas is related and use this information to create a concise summary				
N = Never **R** = Rarely **O** = Often **A** = Always				

Checklist of Good Habits

Name _____   Date _____

Unit 3: Great Readers Use What They Know				
Does the Student:	**N**	**R**	**O**	**A**
Activating Background Knowledge				
Identify the topic of a book				
Generate background knowledge about the topic				
Identify a purpose for reading				
Implement various previewing techniques to determine which aspect of background knowledge is most important and helpful				
Match background knowledge to the topic				
Recognize that the kind of background knowledge he or she needs can change throughout a book according to the subject matter				
Ask questions and look for answers during reading				
Recognize new information while reading, and revise background knowledge to accommodate this new information				
Making Connections				
Recognize when he or she connects to the text				
Connect the text to his or her own experiences and knowledge				
Connect the text to other texts that he or she has read				
Make text-to-world connections while reading				
Use text-to-self, text-to-text, and text-to-world connections to gain a better understanding of the text				
Making Inferences				
Use text clues and background knowledge to make valid inferences				
Know how to use inferences to help clarify the text				
Recognize inferences that need to be revised or expanded and change them to make them more accurate or complete				
N = Never **R** = Rarely **O** = Often **A** = Always				

Checklist of Good Habits

Name _____ Date _____

Unit 4: Great Readers Understand How Stories Work				
Does the Student:	**N**	**R**	**O**	**A**
Understanding Story Elements				
Use visual clues and text features to preview the text				
Identify the story elements of characters, setting, and plot				
Identify the point of view and tell from which perspective the story is told				
Make and revise predictions based on previews, story elements, and point of view				
Understanding and Analyzing Characters				
Distinguish between main characters and minor characters in the story				
Identify the character's purpose for being in the story				
Use what the character says and does to analyze and understand the character				
Describe changes in the character as the plot develops				
Understanding Setting and Plot				
Use both text and illustrations to identify details of a setting				
Know how to use the setting of a story to learn more about the characters				
Use a story map to analyze the plot structure of a story				
Understanding and Analyzing Theme				
Identify with characters and events in the story using text-to-self and text-to-world connections				
Identify one or more valid themes for the story				
Relate the theme of the story to his or her own life in meaningful ways				
N = Never **R** = Rarely **O** = Often **A** = Always				

Checklist of Good Habits

Name _____ Date _____

Unit 5: <u>Great Readers Read to Learn</u>				
Does the Student:	**N**	**R**	**O**	**A**
Making Inferences From Nonfiction				
Pause occasionally to consider how facts stated by the author might reveal additional unstated information				
Recognize the need to make inferences based on information from the author that is implied but not directly stated				
Use prior knowledge and facts from the text to make inferences				
Recognize when an inference needs to be revised and revise it				
Identifying and Using Text Features				
Identify facts from visual sources and use them to enhance understanding of the text				
Know how to combine clues from visual sources with text clues and background knowledge to make inferences				
Evaluate the usefulness of visual sources and tell why they are included				
Identifying and Using Text Structures				
Identify the structure of a text				
Recognize the connection between text structure and author's purpose				
Understand that authors often use more than one structure in a text				
Identify the way in which the structure of a text changes and why				
Evaluating Nonfiction				
Ask questions about the author				
Evaluate the information for accuracy				
Evaluate the text and text features for clarity				
Use evidence from the text or from other resources to support his or her opinions about accuracy and clarity				
N = Never	**R** = Rarely	**O** = Often	**A** = Always	

Checklist of Good Habits

Name _____ Date _____

Unit 6: Great Readers Monitor and Keep Track of Ideas and Information				
Does the Student:	N	R	O	A
Taking Notes on Fiction				
Describe the function of various graphic organizers				
Select an appropriate graphic organizer to match the text and purpose for reading				
Record information according to the format of the selected graphic organizer				
Use the information on a graphic organizer to better understand and make evaluations about story elements				
Evaluate information recorded on a graphic organizer				
Taking Notes on Nonfiction				
Select a graphic organizer based on the text and task				
Differentiate between important and less important ideas and details				
Use the graphic organizer appropriately and efficiently to take notes				
Use key words and phrases to take notes rather than complete sentences				
Put together notes from the graphic organizer to create a comprehensive, cohesive summary				
Self-Monitoring				
Pause to ask questions during reading to monitor comprehension				
Identify key words and ideas related to the main idea				
Reread to regain meaning of important ideas				
Retrace his or her reading to regain lost meaning				
Visualizing				
Pause to visualize information while reading				
Call on prior experiences and background knowledge to form mental and sensory images				
Use an author's descriptive phrases to create mental and sensory images				
Modify mental and sensory images as he or she continues to read				
Tell why visualizing is an important strategy to use when he or she reads				
N = Never **R** = Rarely **O** = Often **A** = Always				

Checklist of Good Habits

Name _____ Date _____

Unit 7: <u>Great Readers Think Critically About Books</u>				
Does the Student:	**N**	**R**	**O**	**A**
Questioning the Commonplace in a Text				
Identify heroes and villains in a story and tell how the behavior of those characters varies from archetypal behavior				
Identify the roles of men and women in a story and recognize how those roles differ from what might be expected				
Identify the ways in which characters in a story treat other characters based on gender stereotypes				
Identify the status of characters and recognize how status affects a character's power and how the character is treated by others				
Considering the Role of the Author				
Identify possible sources of information that an author uses to write a story or a nonfiction text				
Identify material that might be factual in a piece of fiction				
Recognize possible motives that an author might have for writing				
Explain how characters represent the author's message				
Seeking Alternative Perspectives				
Understand the term *perspective*				
Identify the perspectives of different characters in a text				
Retell a story from another character's perspective				
Explain the historical or cultural influences on a book				
Compare and contrast alternative perspectives between texts				
Reading Critically				
Recognize bias demonstrated by a person in a book or by the author of a text				
Recognize when bias is harmful to others				
Identify gaps in information in text and explain how to learn more				
Form and support value judgments, or opinions, about what he or she reads				
N = Never **R** = Rarely **O** = Often **A** = Always				

What is a portfolio?

Like an artist's portfolio, a student's portfolio is a place to keep the evidence of his or her progress. Portfolios include samples of different types of work, carefully chosen by the student in partnership with the teacher. Most portfolios include recordings of students' reading and writing, and even samples selected from speaking and listening activities. Samples should demonstrate development and goal acquisition and should be collected regularly and systematically.

Portfolios involve students in self-assessment, as they select the work to include. Students can include a written reflection of what each entry demonstrates and why it was included in the portfolio.

Portfolios can help you and your students keep track of student learning. They can be integrated into the curriculum and do not take additional instructional time, as traditional assessment tools often do. Portfolios provide a record of student work done over a period of time and support the monitoring of progress toward specified goals. They also help you meet standards, thus fulfilling accountability requirements.

How can a portfolio help you assess students on an ongoing basis?

Because the artifacts collected in the portfolio clearly demonstrate students' growth over time, portfolios become an important informal assessment tool that helps you make ongoing instructional decisions. They are also useful conference tools for discussion with students and parents. More importantly, portfolios encourage students to take pride in their development as readers, to learn more about evaluating their own progress, and to set new learning goals.

How do *Celebration Press Reading: Good Habits, Great Readers* materials support your use of portfolios?

Periodically, help students select at least one of the following to include in a student portfolio:

- work generated during literacy center or independent activities
- assessment forms such as Running Records, checklists, and rubrics that are included in this Assessment Handbook
- graphic organizers generated during Guided and Shared Reading lessons
- work generated during the writing portion of Guided Reading lessons
- recorded summaries or recorded portions of the Talk Together section of Shared Reading lessons
- work completed during the Apply the Strategy portion of Shared Reading lessons
- journal entries completed during Shared and/or Guided Reading lessons

How can you help students choose samples to include in their portfolios?

At the beginning of the year, explain the portfolio process to students. Tell them their portfolios should include:

- samples that demonstrate learning and improvement over time
- samples of "quality work"
- samples that show evidence that students challenged themselves

Explain that it should be clear to anyone looking through their portfolio why students chose to include particular samples. They can use a Portfolio Selection Slip (p. 58) to do this. Encourage students to include on their form reasons for inclusion of the sample and a description of how it speaks to the quality of their work.

How can you use portfolios to help you with the grading process?

Hold portfolio conferences near the end of each grading period to help students reflect on the samples in their portfolio and set goals for the next period's work. You can use the Portfolio Checklist on page 59 to make sure each student's portfolio is organized and up-to-date.

Portfolio Selection Slip

Name _____ Date _____

I chose this piece of work because

_____

_____

_____

_____

_____

_____

This best represents my reading growth because

_____

_____

_____

_____

_____

_____

Portfolio Checklist

Name _____   Date _____

Form	Date(s) Submitted
Summary Rubric	
Story Frame	
Text Frame	
Running Record	
Independent Reading Behaviors Checklist	
Guided Reading Discussion Checklist	
Reading Log	
Checklist of Good Habits	
Home Reading Record	
Checklist of Guided Reading Skills	

Record of Student's Work	

Reporting Progress

What are the purposes of progress reporting?

The goals of progress reporting are to:

- support and motivate students' learning
- identify whether or not students are reading on grade level
- identify whether students are becoming independent, fluent readers
- make students aware of their progress
- inform others regarding students' achievements

What are some general guidelines to follow when reporting students' progress?

- Performance expectations should be clear to students. Explain the criteria for scoring and grading, and provide students with scored models of assignments and testing items.
- Scores and grades should communicate students' achievement in relation to clear and public learning standards.
- A combination of scores, grades, and feedback is useful in improving students' learning goals.

What are some examples of material you can use to monitor progress?

Scoring a variety of students' work ensures a holistic assessment of each student. It is not necessary to score all students' work. You may require that students complete work to practice a concept without providing them with a score. The following materials, however, are excellent vehicles on which to base a score:

- An evaluation of daily class work allows you to check for understanding.
- Students have varying learning styles, so visual (art work), auditory (partner discussions), and kinesthetic (games, pantomime) activities provide them with opportunities to demonstrate learning through a variety of modalities.
- Scoring writing pieces enables you to understand a student's thinking process and assess his or her use of writing strategies.
- Scores on *DRA2* and the *Celebration Press Reading: Good Habits, Great Readers* Assessment Card provide you with an occasion to monitor a student's ability in reading sub-skills and to provide instruction at an appropriate level. Comparing assessment scores over time enhances your ability to track a student's growth.
- Scores on Running Records, Summary Rubrics, and Story and Text Frames provide information about a student's oral reading, comprehension, and understanding of text organization, and can help you tailor instruction to meet each student's needs and monitor his or her progress.
- Scores on surveys and inventories provide information about students' reading behaviors, attitudes, interests, and abilities. This data is useful for planning future instruction.
- Portfolios allow you to track a student's growth in the various components of reading over time and share information about a student with parents, school administrators, and other school personnel who work with the student, and with the student, too.

What opportunities for reporting progress are provided in *Celebration Press Reading: Good Habits, Great Readers?*

Analyzing a variety of students' work will enable you to provide accurate grades for students, parents, teachers, and others. You can analyze the following items and tasks that are part of *Celebration Press Reading: Good Habits, Great Readers*:

- participation in Shared Reading Focus Lessons
- participation in Guided Reading groups
- writing activities in Guided Reading lessons
- participation in Shared Reading Mini-lesson activities
- work generated during Shared Reading Wrap-up activities
- partner discussions during Shared Reading lessons
- Running Records (p. 39)
- Summary Rubrics (p. 31)
- Story and Text Frames (pp. 33, 34)
- Home Reading Record (p. 64)
- components of student's portfolio

How can the assessment components in *Celebration Press Reading: Good Habits, Great Readers* help you determine letter grades?

Numeric grades are generally determined by dividing a student's score on a task by the total possible score. Letter grades, however, tend to reflect a variety of information—much of it gleaned from assessment. Benchmark Assessment Books used in *DRA2* and other formative assessments often compare to grade-level expectations, and they can help you determine how students are progressing through the developmental stages of reading. In addition, information assessment checks in both Shared and Guided Reading are provided to help you understand how well a student is grasping strategies.

There are other measures of progress, as well. Shared Reading work can help you observe progress in a whole-group setting, while individual effort in learning centers and guided reading groups can also contribute to a letter grade. The checklists provided in this Assessment Handbook provide a more concrete list of skill-based tasks that teachers can use as evidence that strategies and skills are being mastered. All of this information can then be combined to assign a letter grade to student performance based on grade-level expectations.

It is important for uniformity and accuracy that teachers in a school or a district apply grades consistently. If your school or district does not have grading guidelines, or the guidelines are outdated, suggest the formation of a committee to address this issue.

How do you measure progress at the end of a Shared Reading unit?

Evidence of application of the strategies taught in each unit can and should be measured through ongoing progress monitoring. The Checklists of Good Habits on pages 49–55 are an excellent record-keeping tool for this purpose.

Meeting Individual Needs

How does *Celebration Press Reading: Good Habits, Great Readers* support English language learners?

The *Celebration Press Reading: Good Habits, Great Readers* classroom is an excellent place for English language learners to develop both content knowledge and literacy skills. The scaffolding and gradual release of responsibility throughout the program provide critical differentiated instruction in both whole-class and small-group learning.

In Shared Reading lessons, ESL/ELL Support suggestions appear at the end of each week. The suggested activities address the needs of English language learners by including an alternative way of approaching the week's key strategy. Lesson strategies appropriate for increasing the understanding of students who are learning English are suggested. These include the use of visualizing, verbalizing, hands-on activities, sorting and classifying activities, breaking the strategy into concrete steps, and using real-life examples.

In Guided Reading, a short activity or series of questions to address a specific ESL/ELL issue is included in the ESL/ELL Support portion of the lesson. It may be an instructional tip or activity to help students better understand concepts, such as the meaning of a word. In some cases, the lesson focuses on a critical concept from the book. For example, if the book deals with celebrations around the world, the word *holiday* or *celebration* would be a critical concept to understand in order to attempt to read the book.

How does *Celebration Press Reading: Good Habits, Great Readers* support students with special needs?

Using *Celebration Press Reading: Good Habits, Great Readers* to meet the needs of students with special needs is very similar to meeting the needs of all students. The program offers flexibility in placing students in the text level that will best meet their instructional needs.

It is likely that students with special needs may be a part of *Celebration Press Reading: Good Habits, Great Readers* Guided Reading groups. Teachers should carefully match instruction to the information gleaned from the assessment results. For example, teachers may want to

- place additional instructional emphasis on the featured reading skill by more carefully monitoring progress of the special-needs student or by providing additional practice with the same skill as the student moves to independent reading later

- use Shared Reading activities to further emphasize the instructional needs of students

- move the student to address the strategies and skills in a lower-level text for Guided Reading using additional lessons provided on the *Celebration Press Reading: Good Habits, Great Readers* Web site (**www.goodhabitsgreatreaders.com**)

- partner the special-needs student with a classmate who has already mastered the targeted reading skill so the student has a role model available

- begin daily lessons with a quick review of the instructional skill emphasized on the previous day

In all cases, students with special needs benefit from a tight link between assessment and instruction, careful review of newly acquired skills, and reinforcement for progress made. And, as with all students, students with special needs benefit by having their newly acquired skills labeled as they are learning them. This helps students build metacognitive awareness and make connections to other, more sophisticated skills as they move through the developmental reading process.

Home-School Connection

How can you use information gleaned from assessment to report reading progress to family members?

Sharing student progress is an important responsibility. The most important message to parents and family members is that reading success is more than a level! As educators, it is our responsibility to always share a student's reading level in the context of our expectations for students at the particular grade level or reading stage.

One suggestion for sharing reading progress is to provide both the reading level and accuracy percentage, along with other information gleaned through the assessment tools found in this Assessment Handbook. These provide a more complete picture of student reading than just a level that is represented by a number or letter grade.

Many schools that use DRA2 as a formative assessment find that the list of characteristics of good readers, located in the front of the DRA2 Teacher Guide, is an excellent resource when providing a report to parents and families. Many parents do not understand that reading is more complex than just good decoding and appreciate the opportunity to review the characteristics. Some school districts provide parents and families with a handout of these characteristics with the DRA2 level and other scores listed right on the same handout. This also provides a great springboard for you to share with parents your focus for instruction for the remainder of the school year and provide suggestions to parents for supporting students at home. In addition, there is no better tool than the DRA2 Continuum to illustrate during parent-teacher conferences the student's personal strengths and needs.

What is a Home Reading Record?

A Home Reading Record is a form on which to chronicle what, how, and when a student is reading at home. A Home Reading Record helps you:

- understand how frequently a student reads at home
- monitor how a student reads at home
- compare and contrast school and home reading habits
- respond to the questions or concerns of family members

How do you use it?

- Send home with students a blank Home Reading Record such as the one shown on page 64, along with the instructional letter on page 65.
- Establish a schedule for reviewing these Home Reading Records.
- Refer to the record during the parent-teacher conference.

Home Reading Record

Name _____

Date	Title and Author	Comments	Initials

64 **Assessment Handbook Grades 4/5**

Dear Family Members,

Please talk to your child frequently about his or her reading. This will give your child practice with the skills he or she is learning at school. It will also improve your child's understanding and fluency, as well as promote greater enjoyment of reading.

Allow your child to select appropriate reading materials from the school or local library. Encourage frequent use of the library and good habits in book handling and in keeping track of and returning books. Books can be listened to as well as read—books on tape or audio CD are a good way for reluctant readers to engage more fully with text.

Once your child has read a book, encourage him or her to talk about the experience with you. You do not have to read the book yourself; instead, have your child tell you what he or she liked and/or didn't like about the book. You may want to encourage your child to consider reading more books on a certain topic or by a specific author.

Please make this sharing time a relaxing and enjoyable experience for you and your child. While you may want to discuss the book, you will want to refrain from asking too many questions every time he or she reads.

Have your child record his or her home reading sessions on the attached Home Reading Record, and then initial the Record and have your child return it to school so that we may discuss it at our parent-teacher conferences. Thank you for your help and support.

Sincerely,

Appendix

Questions for Reading Conferences

Unit 1: Great Readers See Themselves as Readers

Choosing Books

- How can thinking about favorite books and authors help you find new books to enjoy?

- How can a book's cover help you decide if the book might be of interest to you?

- What are some types of reading materials you enjoy? What are some new reading materials you might try?

- How are you going to use a purpose for reading to influence your book choice?

- What are some books that you read some time ago that are still important to you? Why are they important? How have they helped make you the reader you are today?

- What are some interesting books that you have recently discovered? What makes those books of interest to you?

Building Reading Stamina

- How can setting a goal to read more challenging texts make reading more fun or interesting for you?

- When you are reading, what are some signs that you are stuck on something? What are some strategies you know how to use to get unstuck?

- Why is building stamina as a reader important to becoming a better reader?

- How can setting a goal to read longer books make you a more proficient reader?

- Suppose you come to something in the text that you don't understand or were unsure about. What are some strategies that can aid your understanding?

- How do you plan to meet your goals for becoming a better reader?

Appendix

Unit 2: Great Readers Make Sense of Text

Making Predictions

- What experiences have you had that can help you make predictions about this part of the text?

- How can you use text structure or text features to make a prediction about what you will learn on these pages?

- How can making predictions help you better understand a text?

Asking Questions

- What questions can you ask to check your understanding of what you are reading? Where can you find the answers in the text?

- What do you wonder about in this part of the text? How can you use text clues and your own knowledge and experience to answer your questions?

- How does asking questions throughout reading help you better understand a text?

- What questions could you ask to help you predict events or information?

- Why do you think it is important to formulate questions you would like to ask the author?

- How does asking yourself questions help you understand the text?

- When is it important to ask yourself questions about what you are reading?

Clarifying

- Why is it important to learn strategies that help you clarify what you read?

- Which strategy do you think is the most helpful when you want to clarify the meaning of a word? Why?

- Which strategy do you find most helpful when you want to clarify the meaning of a concept? Why?

- How does using your prior knowledge help you clarify meaning?

Summarizing and Synthesizing

- When you pause to think about what you have read, what do you do first? Next? Then? How will this help you as a reader?

- How can you decide which details are important to the main idea, and which are not?

- What other strategies do you already know how to use that can help you learn to summarize? (for example, recognizing sequence of events, identifying key words, and using text features such as headings)

Appendix

Unit 3: Great Readers Use What They Know

Activating Background Knowledge

- Why is it important to identify the topic of a book and what you already know about the topic?

- How can thinking about your purpose for reading help you figure out what information you'll need to understand the text?

- What did you learn by previewing text features, such as the title, cover, chapter headings, and graphs and charts?

- How does focusing on the most important background knowledge and activating this knowledge before reading a text make you a better reader?

- Why might the background knowledge you need during reading change from one chapter to another?

- How can asking questions as you read help you focus on the text?

- How does your background knowledge change when you discover new information while reading?

- How does activating appropriate background knowledge make you a better reader?

- How can recording what you know about a topic on a web or chart help you learn something new as you read?

- What should you do with the new information you discover while reading?

Making Connections

- How does this part of the text remind you of something from your own life?

- What other texts remind you of this text? How can you connect the two texts?

- What are some connections you can make between this text and the world around you?

- How can making connections help you as a reader?

Making Inferences

- Why is it important to figure out parts of a text that are not stated directly in a text?

- How can making an inference help clear up confusion you have about a text?

- What can you do if you make an inference that turns out to be incomplete or incorrect?

- When should you revise or expand an inference?

- How can making inferences help you better understand what you are reading?

Appendix

Unit 4: Great Readers Understand How Stories Work

Understanding Story Elements

- Why is it important to preview a story? What do you notice in your preview?

- What are some important story elements in this story?

- What is the point of view in this story? What were the clues you used to identify the point of view?

- How can understanding story elements make you a better reader?

Understanding and Analyzing Characters

- How do you know which characters are the main characters in this story?

- Why does the author include each character in the story? What purposes do the characters have?

- How would you describe this character? What does the character say or do to support your opinion?

- How does this character change as the plot develops?

- How does analyzing and understanding characters help you as a reader?

Understanding Setting and Plot

- Where and when does the story take place? What details make the setting interesting?

- How can you use the setting of the story to help you learn more about the character(s)?

- What are the five parts of a plot? What happens in each part? How can you keep track of a plot?

- Why is it important for readers to identify the setting and keep track of the plot as they read?

Understanding and Analyzing Theme

- How can you relate to the characters in this story, as well as to the things that happen to them?

- What does the author want you to know or learn from reading this story?

- How does the theme of this story relate to your own life?

- How does identifying with characters and events, as well as the theme of a story, help you better understand the story you are reading? How does it help you better understand life around you?

Appendix

Unit 5: Great Readers Read to Learn

Locating Facts and Information

- What information do the title, cover, and contents page give you about a book?

- Why is it a good idea to look up boldfaced words in the glossary before reading them in the text?

- What are some reasons for using an index to locate information about a specific topic in other places in a book, rather than check the contents page or other pages in the book?

- How does using nonfiction text features to locate facts and information help you read nonfiction text more efficiently and with greater understanding?

Making Inferences From Nonfiction

- How can you use facts that are stated directly by the author to figure out other information that is not stated directly?

- Why do you think authors don't include every detail but expect the reader to make inferences?

- How can you use what you already know to help you make inferences?

- What do you do if you make an inference that turns out to need revision?

- How can making inferences as you read help you read with purpose and focus your thinking?

- Why can't you expect that all the inferences you make while reading will be correct?

Identifying and Using Text Features

- What visual sources are included in this text? What important factual information can you gain from this visual?

- How can you use the information from this visual source along with text clues and your own knowledge and experience to make an inference?

- How useful is this visual source? Why do you think the author includes it in the text?

- How does using visual sources help you better understand the texts that you read?

Identifying and Using Text Structures

- What text structure does the author use in this part of the text?

- What is the author's purpose for writing this part of the text? How does the text structure fit the author's purpose?

- What are the different structures used on these pages? Where does the text structure change? How do you know it changes?

- How can learning about text structure help you better understand the nonfiction texts that you read?

Appendix

Evaluating Nonfiction

- What questions would you ask about this author?

- How would you check the accuracy of this information?

- What helps you decide if the information is clear and easy to understand?

- Would you recommend this book to someone who wants to learn about this subject? Why or why not?

Unit 6: Great Readers Monitor and Keep Track of Ideas and Information

Taking Notes on Fiction

- What type of graphic organizer would help you gain a deeper understanding of this text? Why?

- How does using this graphic organizer help you keep track of information in the book you are reading?

- What new information did you notice when you created a graphic organizer about [character's name]?

- How does using an appropriate graphic organizer to note information as you read a story or a novel help make you a better reader?

Taking Notes on Nonfiction

- How can previewing the contents page help you decide what type of graphic organizer will work best?

- What clues do authors give readers to let them know which ideas and details are important?

- What is the most efficient way to record notes from the text on a graphic organizer?

- How do you think taking notes on a graphic organizer can make summarizing easier for you?

- How does knowing how to take notes on nonfiction text make you a better reader?

Self-Monitoring

- What are some ways you can identify key words in a text?

- How does identifying key words and ideas help you focus on the main idea?

- What questions might you ask to monitor your comprehension? How would you find the answers?

Appendix

Unit 6: Great Readers Monitor and Keep Track of Ideas and Information (continued)

- How does asking questions about the text help you monitor your comprehension?

- Suppose you lost meaning of a text you were reading. What would you do?

- How does monitoring your understanding while you read help make you a better reader?

- How does rereading help you understand the text?

Visualizing

- What do you use to help you create mental and sensory images when you read a piece of text?

- What words or phrases most help you visualize?

- What mental and sensory images do you visualize when you read this part of the text?

- How do your visualizations change when you read new text about the same subject?

- How does visualizing help you when you read?

Unit 7: Great Readers Think Critically About Books

Questioning the Commonplace in a Text

- Who is the hero in this story? Who is the villain? What behaviors do they demonstrate that do not fit those roles?

- How is the behavior of the men and women in this story different from what might be expected? Why do you think they act this way?

- How are characters in this story misjudged because of their gender? What is the truth about who they are or what they do in the story?

- How would you describe the wealth and class of the characters in this story? How does wealth and class determine how much power the characters have or how others treat them?

- What questions might you ask yourself about characters and their status in a story? How can you become a better reader by questioning things that some readers might take for granted?

Considering the Role of the Author

- What library reference sources might the author have used? Who could the author have interviewed to get accurate information?

- What are some possible motives the author might have had for writing this selection? Why do you think that?

- What character traits do the characters in this story display? How do the characters represent the author's message?

- How can thinking about the role of an author help you better understand a reading selection and an author's reasons for writing it?

Seeking Alternative Perspectives

- Why is it possible for two characters in a book to view the same event differently?

- What is the perspective of the main character? How is that perspective the same as or different from other characters' perspectives?

- What historical influences can you identify that influence this text?

- What are some cultural influences on this text? Why might a story make sense in one part of the world, but not another?

- How do the perspective and purpose of this text compare with those of another text on a similar topic?

- Why is it a good idea to use more than one source to evaluate information? Why might authors writing about the same thing provide different information?

- How can looking for different perspectives help you better understand what you are reading?

Reading Critically

- What are one or more examples of bias in this text? What is your opinion of the bias? Do you think this is an example of a harmful bias? Why?

- What information is missing from a text that you are reading? What would you like to learn more about? Where could you look to get more information?

- What do you agree with in this text? Why?

- What do you disagree with in this text? Why?

- How can thinking critically about and evaluating what an author writes make you a better reader?

Appendix

Guided Reading Skills Checklist

Name _____ Date _____

Guided Reading Skills	Proficient	Developing	Having Difficulty	Not Showing Trait
Analyze Character				
Analyze Setting				
Analyze Theme				
Categorize and Classify				
Compare and Contrast				
Determine Cause and Effect				
Determine Main Ideas and Details				
Determine Problem and Solution				
Draw Conclusions				
Make Connections				
Make Inferences				
Monitor Comprehension				
Recognize Author's Purpose				
Recognize Point of View				
Summarize				
Understand Genre				
Understand Mood				
Understand Nonfiction Text Structure:				
Cause and Effect				
Compare/Contrast				
Description				
Problem and Solution				
Sequence of Events				
Steps in a Process				
Understand Plot				
Understand Sequence of Events				
Use Nonfiction Features				
Visualize				

Bibliography/Recommended Reading

Bear, D. R., Invernizzi, M., Templeton, S., & Johnson, F. (2004). *Words their way: Word study for phonics, vocabulary, and spelling instruction.* Upper Saddle River, NJ: Pearson Education.

Beaver, J. M. (2006). *Developmental reading assessment second edition (DRA2).* Parsippany, NJ: Celebration Press.

Benson, V., & Cummins, C. (2004). *The power of retelling: Developmental steps for building comprehension.* Bothell, WA: McGraw-Hill.

Caldwell, J. S., & Leslie, L. (2005). *Intervention strategies to follow: Informal reading inventory assessment.* Boston, MA: Pearson Education.

Center for the Improvement of Early Reading Achievement (CIERA). (2001). *Put reading first: The research building blocks for teaching children to read.* Washington, DC: U.S. Department of Education, Partnership for Reading.

Chang, K., Sung, Y., & Chen, I. (2002). The effect of concept mapping to enhance text comprehension and summarization. *Journal of Experimental Education, 71,* 5–23.

Clay, M. M. (1985). *The early detection of reading difficulties: A diagnostic survey with recovery procedures (3rd ed.).* Auckland, New Zealand, Heinemann.

Clay, M. M. (1991). *Becoming literate: The construction of inner control.* Portsmouth, NH: Heinemann.

Cunningham, P. M., & Allington, R. L. (2003). *Classrooms that work: They can all read and write.* Boston, MA: Pearson Education.

Duke, N. K., & Bennett-Armistead, S. (2003). *Reading and writing informational text in the primary grades.* New York, NY: Scholastic Inc.

Frey, N., & Fisher, D. B. (2006). *Language arts workshop: Purposeful reading and writing instruction.* Upper Saddle River, NJ: Pearson Education.

Hoyt, L. (2002). *Make it real: Strategies for success with informational texts.* Portsmouth, NH: Heinemann.

Kamil, M. L., Mosenthal, P. B., Pearson, P. B., Pearson, P. D., & Barr, R. (Eds.). (2000). *Handbook of reading research (Vol. 3).* Mahwah, NJ: Erlbaum.

Keene, E. O., & Zimmermann, S. (1997). *Mosaic of thought: Teaching comprehension in a reader's workshop.* Portsmouth, NH: Heinemann.

Kristo, J. V., & Bamford, R. A. (2004). *Nonfiction in focus: A comprehensive framework for helping students become independent readers and writers of nonfiction, K–6.* New York, NY: Scholastic Inc.

National Institute of Child Health and Human Development (NICHD). (2000). *Report of the National Reading Panel. Teaching children to read: An evidence-based assessment of the scientific research literature on reading and its implications for reading instruction* (NIH Publication No. 00-4769). Washington, DC: U.S. Government Printing Office.

National Research Council (NRC). (2002). *Scientific research in education* (Report of the Committee on Scientific Principles for Education Research). Washington, DC: National Academy Press.

No Child Left Behind Act of 2001, Pub. L. No. 107-110, 155 Stat. 1425 (2002).

Opitz, M. F., & Ford, M. P. (2001). *Reaching readers: Flexible and innovative strategies for guided reading.* Portsmouth, NH: Heinemann.

Parkes, B. (2000). *Read it again!: Revisiting shared reading.* Portland ME: Stenhouse Publishers.

Payne, C. D. (2005). *Shared reading for today's classroom.* New York, NY: Scholastic Inc.

Pinnell, G. S., & Fountas, I. C. (1999). *Matching books to readers: Using leveled books in guided reading, K–3.* Portsmouth, NH: Heinemann.

Schulman, M. B., & Payne, C. D. (2000). *Guided reading: Making it work.* New York, NY: Scholastic Inc.

Snow, C. E., Burns, M. S., & Griffin, P. (Eds.). (1998). *Preventing reading difficulties in young children.* Washington, DC: National Academy Press.

Strickland, K. (2005). *What's after assessment?: Follow-up instructions for phonics, fluency and comprehension.* Portsmouth, NH: Heinemann.

Swartz, S. L., Shook, R. E., & Klein, A. F. (2002). *Shared reading: Reading with children.* Carlsbad, CA: Dominie Press.

Swartz, S. L., Shook, R. E., Klein, A. F., Moon, C., Bunnell, K., Belt, M., & Huntley, C. (2003). *Guided reading and literacy centers.* Carlsbad, CA: Dominie Press.

Taberski, S. (2000). *On solid ground: Strategies for teaching reading K–3.* Portsmouth, NH: Heinemann.

My Notes

My Notes

My Notes

My Notes